HOW TO FAKE
ROMANCE
(When Your Love Is Real)

Martin VanWoudenberg

iUniverse, Inc.
Bloomington

How to Fake Romance
(When Your Love is Real)

iUniverse books may be ordered through booksellers or by contacting:

iUniverse
1663 Liberty Drive
Bloomington, IN 47403
www.iuniverse.com
1-800-Authors (1-800-288-4677)

ISBN: 978-1-4502-5738-1 (pbk)
ISBN: 978-1-4502-5737-4 (ebk)
ISBN: 978-1-4502-5739-8 (hbk)

Library of Congress Control Number: 2010913324

Printed in the United States of America

iUniverse rev. date: 11/09/10

For Nicole,
who gives me a reason for all of this

Contents

Introduction: What's All This About?

Ah, romance ... that mysterious and wonderful thing about which poets write, musicians sing, actors perform, and your partner keeps nagging you—that intangible thing. It has no physical substance (unlike a truck), cannot be eaten (unlike a steak), and cannot be bought (unlike a new stereo). Yet, somehow, a man is expected to possess it in limitless quantities, and to know just what it is, how it works, and when and how to use it. After all, it is called ro*man*ce, isn't it?

Fear not, help is here. Despite the fact that romance is not taught in school and cannot really be learned, there is a way to fake it well enough to get away with it. Nobody really knows what this romance thing is. Those who do claim to know about it—I do when I'm showing off at parties—probably are lying; they just fake it better than the average person. Romance is like anything else in life; all you need to do is practice long enough and hard enough, and you will become an expert. Romance is a bit like magic. Those who impress us with their ability to make coins go through tables and elephants disappear in the desert are not truly magical. They possess no inherent power. They simply fake magic better than we do. The same is true of romance. We will learn to fake it well enough to fool the uneducated observer. And by that, though I mean no disrespect, I mean your partner.

Before I get into the actual "help" part, there are a few important things to discuss. Without the answers to these questions, you will not find value in this book. I do not want you to feel like you have been misled. No matter what happens in the future, you must realize the value of learning a little about, and learning to cope with, this romance thing.

Answering a few questions, will help you learn to use this book's system properly and get the desired results.

Let's get right into it, shall we?

1) What fool started this whole romance thing in the first place?

After God created the world and put Adam in it, he decided that man needed someone to help him. Since there was no suitable helper available, God created woman. Adam awoke to find Eve present (and one of his ribs missing, but that is another issue altogether). He promptly said, "Wow, baby, you look amazing!" (or something to that effect), and romance was born.

Eve decided she liked getting compliments, and soon Adam was providing them on everything from her hair to the curvature of her toes. Of course, with that came Eden's flowers, cards made from tree bark, and the promises of undying love. Eve taught her daughters about this great thing called romance, but Adam was not smart enough to talk to his sons about it and nip the whole thing in the bud. Things got worse from there.

2) Is this Adam fellow still living? Can get some of the guys together so we can beat him up?

No, Adam died, as do most men when they spend their lives trying to please women. Eve eventually died too.

3) Since they are dead, does anyone care about romance anymore?

Remember Eve's daughters? Well, they all had daughters too. And those daughters had daughters as well. Catching on yet? Today, there are millions and millions of daughters, all thinking this romance thing is a really cool idea. Your partner is one of them.

4) Since she is already my partner, why do I need romance?

This is a tough question to answer. When you were courting your partner, you saw the value in romance. Your love for her was sincere, but you didn't think she'd believe you unless you also faked a romantic nature. She chose you, delighting in getting one of the few men who "understood" the importance of the "little things." Once the honeymoon period was over, you figured the show was over, and you could start being yourself. Unfortunately, that did not go over too well with your partner. Women have this strange little thing; they do not like being deceived. Men generally love it when they are lied to, as long as it sounds good. But women are different.

Your partner expects you to continue romancing her even after you've made the commitment. What is the point?, you ask. Just take a look at someone who continues to romance his partner after everything becomes official and routine, and you will likely see something different about him. See that silly grin? Remember the last time you had that grin on your face? Perhaps it has been so long that you cannot remember.

Of course, romance also makes your partner feel loved, helps you express yourself more deeply, draws you closer as a couple, makes you less likely to find the mailman in your bedroom, and gives you many other benefits.

5) Are there any statistics, studies, or books that prove that?

Actually, there are a great many books, studies, and very detailed statistics that prove this. A simple walk through a bookstore will show you the huge selection of available books on love, romance, sex (see, this is not all bad), and other matters of the heart. If you are interested,

I can recommend a short list of fifty to a hundred of the best titles. No time to read fifty books? I thought so.

6) *How can I deal with this romance stuff? This sounds serious.*

This is the real beauty of this book. Unlike many other books on this subject, this one does not pretend to try to teach you how to be real romantic. You won't have to read long pages on the art of romance, the history of romance, and so on. All you need to do is follow a few basic steps, and you're all set. Guaranteed.

7) *Will she catch on to this faking thing?*

Absolutely not! This book is going to teach you how to fake romance so well that you will convince not only your partner but her entire family as well. In fact, if you follow the steps properly and make just the slightest bit of effort, you may even convince yourself. It is just like magic, remember? Your romantic sleight of hand will feel like genuine wizardry to the observer.

Of course, if you really work on these techniques and perfect every nuance, there's a danger you might become a real romantic! We don't want that to happen, however, so we'll ensure that you do just the right amount and don't endanger your manly man status.

8) *Really? Cool! Is it hard to do?*

It is very easy to do. If you can read (please tell me you are not just looking for the pictures) and you can write (printing is fine too), then you can fake your way through romance. Occasionally you will need to fold, tape, and staple as well, but we'll try to keep those activities to a bare minimum.

9) Okay, then; but I bet it's really expensive, right?

Other than the cost of this book, there is minimal cost. The few basic supplies that you will need should cost you less than a large pizza, and some are totally free.

10) If it is cheap, it must take a long time to do. Correct?

Wrong again. Most of the romantic ideas and activities in this book will take less time than a TV commercial. (Of course, the really short commercial breaks do not count.) A few items will take longer, but since I am sensitive about your time, I have kept those to a minimum.

11) Are you are sure I can do this during commercial breaks?

Yes. It has been tried by many, and it works.

12) Where do I sign up?

At the next section. Venture forth, dear reader.

Quick Start Guide: How Do We Do This?

We are now ready to get down to the real "meat" (or tofu, if you are vegetarian) of this book. In this section, we will go over a little more (just a wee bit more) about why this is so important, how to properly fake the romance thing, and how to use this book to maximum effect.

It is very possible that you were given this book by someone who knows you. (People don't usually give books to complete strangers, but anything is possible.) Your feelings about this gift will differ depending on who that person was. You may feel happy, sad, resentful, or just plain puzzled. I am going to try and explain those feelings you are experiencing. If you do not understand the reasons why this book is now in your possession, you may not discover the great ideas it presents, and that would be a real shame.

Keep an open mind (and stay awake); you likely will find that there are rewards aplenty if you make a small bit of effort to relate on a slightly deeper level with your life partner.

How this books works

This section is really important, so do not skip over it. Once you get through the introduction chapters—the endless banter and wit and all the supporting material—you will get to the heart and soul of this book. Like any good instruction manual, it contains information in a short, easy-to-read format. Most men should have no trouble following the instructions.

To fake romance well enough to convince your partner, you need to do something romantic one to three times a month. Let us assume that you will do something specifically romantic for your partner twice a month. There are ninety ideas in this book, organized into easy bite-sized pieces. Assuming that you do one at a time, you will get at least three and a half years of action from the following pages.

Because great ideas can be used more than once, I have placed check boxes on each page and with each idea. Every time you use one of the ideas, place a check in one of the boxes. Once you have used an idea three times, it probably no longer will have the desired effect. Ninety ideas, three times each, twice a month—you will look like a romantic genius for the next ten and a half years. (There's real value for you!)

The ideas themselves are explained in just enough detail to make sense but not in so much detail as to bore you. Each item also lists the supplies that you will need, suggestions for maximizing your impact, and potential pitfalls and traps.

Like a good movie, every main idea also has a supporting cast. With each item you will find secondary ideas that you can throw in at some point during the month. A single romantic gesture is not going to knock your lady off her feet. What you need to do is some other gesture that shows in a simple way that you love, respect, cherish, and honor your lifelong partner (at least for that brief faking period). These supporting ideas may take slightly longer than a commercial break (not significantly longer, though) but when used in combination with the main ideas will be a sure-fire way to bring about the desired results. Wink, wink, nudge, nudge.

There is also a unique added bonus that I guarantee you will not find in any other book on romance (until it catches on and everyone starts to copy it). Every item includes a section of interesting, useful, or just plain entertaining facts about women, food, wars, bizarre laws, technology, and the other really important things in life. How cool is that?

If you stick to the schedule, you will have something interesting and worthwhile to look forward to every few weeks, and your partner will as well.

A few notes about scheduling

Most men today have some sort of date planner, calendar, iPhone, BlackBerry, or other device that keeps track of the things to do during any given week. You will need one of those, and you will need to refer to it on a fairly regular basis. If you are one of the few men who do not use anything to remind them about important events, then it is quite possible that you have missed your anniversary, your partner's birthday, and other crucial happenings. If that is the case, this book most likely will not help you. I suggest that you read it simply for the cool facts and consider visiting a relationship counselor.

If you do use something to keep track of your schedule (or suddenly see the value of doing so), then do the following: Look at every month, and pick a few random days. These chosen days will be the days that you do your romantic thing. Do not pick the same day every week; your partner will see right through that. Women like to be surprised and enjoy maintaining the illusion that men are spontaneous. Since you may need assistance to remember to be spontaneous, I have come up with a system to ensure that you are or at least look like you are.

Put a little note or symbol on the chosen day of the week. Make it something small and nondescript to keep your guy friends in the dark. Or create a symbol that allows you to come up with a story that will make sense if a friend should see it. "That little circle? That's just to remind me to check the tire pressure on the car." The danger here, of course, is that you *will* use that symbol to check the tire pressure rather than on fake romancing your partner. Please remained focused, and this will work.

One more small matter, and we'll be off and running.

Each idea in this book comes with a handy barometer for measuring the potential challenges that lie within an idea. There are three of these measurements: tracking financial cost, the potential for inadvertent disaster, and the time commitment required to pull this off successfully. Each barometer is filled with a toxic and viscous liquid, and as we do not wish this to spill over and mutate us into genuinely romantic people, we will keep a close eye on them. If you are pressed for time, and the next idea on the list reveals that a larger portion of time is going to be required, do not panic. Simply flip ahead to an idea that contains the barometer elements you find most appealing at that particular time, and proceed accordingly. You can always come back to the original idea, and pick it up again later.

Each barometer is labeled for your convenience. An example follows here.

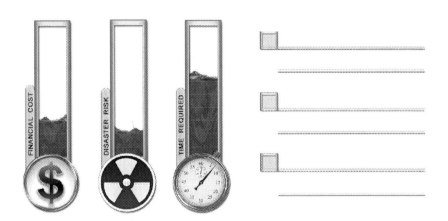

Making It Happen: Let's Do This!

Idea 1: A note on the bathroom mirror

Details

Start simple until you get the hang of this. This week's exercise requires a simple Post-it note and a pen. Write a very simple message to your partner, telling her that you love her. It can be as simple as "I love you, Susan" (if your partner's name is Susan). Put it in a place where she's sure to see it. If you place it on the mirror where she does her hair and makeup, perhaps also refer to a physical feature of hers that you particularly admire.

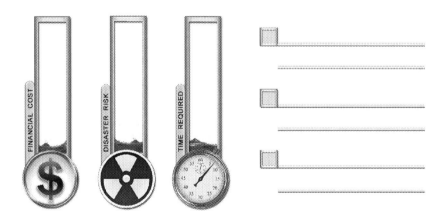

Pitfalls

It is pretty hard to do this one incorrectly, but there are a few things that could detract from your desired impact on this maiden voyage. For one, if your partner's name is Janet, and you write "I love you, Susan," I am fairly sure you will not get a favorable reaction.

Another possible pitfall is if you decide to admire a feature that she does not find attractive or one that she is not able to see in the mirror (we will leave that to your common sense). Similarly, avoid mentioning a feature that you have made her feel self-conscious about in the past. It may not seem as genuine.

Extras

The extra credit this week is also very simple. Each day this week, sometime during the day, anytime will do, tell your partner that you love her. And, this is very important: mean it. I personally like reminding my partner that I love her just before I fall asleep at night. If I die during the night, then at least my last words to her were something positive. (Not to mention that in a few hours I may steal all her covers, roll on top of her, kick her in the shins, or elbow her in the head.) Try it—the saying "I love you" part, not the kicking in the shins—it is worth the effort.

Random Fact 01

The phrase "rule of thumb" is derived from an old English law, which stated that you could not beat your wife with anything wider than your thumb. A crowbar, apparently, is legal then.

Idea 2: A phone message

Details

This idea will require just a wee bit of advance planning and thought. At a time when your partner is not at home, call the house and leave a message for her on the answering machine or voicemail system. If your partner runs errands during the day, works, volunteers, or does anything else that takes her away from the phone for a while, this idea will work.

Leave a very simple message, such as the following:

> Hi, honey. I was thinking about you a lot today and wanted to tell you that I love you. Life is always full of so much stuff; some of it is great and some of it is not so great. You are part of the really great stuff. I love you, sweetheart.

Make sure that your partner is the one that checks the message, rather than one of the kids or your mother-in-law.

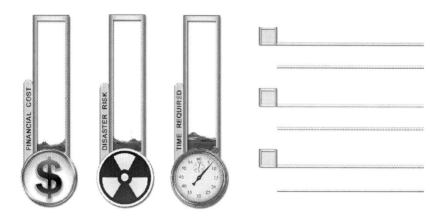

Pitfalls

There are a few ways in which this idea can go wrong. You certainly do not want someone else to check the phone message instead of your partner. The trick here is to know when she is going to be away from the phone and for how long.

The second pitfall could be teasing from friends, coworkers, drinking buddies, or others who think you are getting soft because you leave mushy messages for the love of your life. A solution is to avoid being overheard; leave your message using a cell phone, a pay phone, or a private phone at work.

If you are unable to leave a message or are sincerely afraid that someone else will hear it, then just call her when she is at home. When she answers, tell her you were thinking about her, and then recite the lines above.

Please do not read them out of this book while on the phone; you might sound like a telemarketer, and she'll either hang up on you or ask you if you've fallen and hit your head. If you say it in a natural way, however, she will be impressed.

If none of these ideas sound like they will work, then you can always send her a text. However, the sound of your voice and the added time it takes to plan and make the call are key elements in creating the right effect. If possible, avoid the simplest way.

Random Fact 02

Chrysler built B-29s that bombed Japan. Mitsubishi built Zeros that tried to shoot them down. Both companies now build cars in a joint plant called Diamond Star. Who says we can't all get along?

Extras

This communication thing (telephone or otherwise) is something men usually have to work on a fair bit. Little things in this area can make a big difference. This week, try to remember to call your partner if you are going to be late for dinner, are making plans with friends that may affect her schedule, or will eat a really late lunch and therefore will not want supper. Are you getting the idea?

Idea 3: A single flower

Details

Ever since Adam and Eve spent days walking in a perfect garden, women have had a thing for flowers. Flowers have become an almost universal symbol for love and affection. Like most small tokens, their power rests in the simple fact that you had her on your mind, and you acted on it.

This week, buy (or pick) a single flower and leave it in her car where she can find it. This can be in the morning before she leaves for work or errands. It can be in the evening before she leaves to shop for groceries or visit friends. It can be anytime at all, even when you are going to go somewhere together. Just make sure that the flower is on her seat and that it is in the car before she gets there. The double impact of the gesture and the surprise works well.

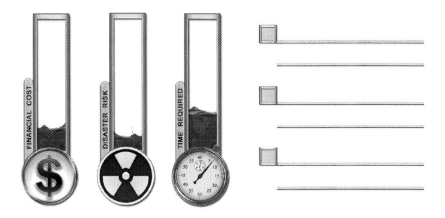

Pitfalls

Please make sure it is the right kind of flower. A red rose symbolizes love and affection, a white rose is for purity, and a yellow rose is for friendship. Tulips, daffodils, carnations, and many other types are all great. However, do not get any flower that is associated with death or your partner may think you want to kill her. Wildflowers can be lovely but be sure you are allowed to pick them. Also make sure that you are not taking some poison oak along with your gift.

If your partner has the habit of throwing things in the car or sitting down before she looks inside, put the flower on the dashboard instead. It would be unfortunate if she sat on the rose thorns. Yes, she will remember the occasion but not in the way you were hoping.

Extras

If you have done this right, and your partner is receptive to tokens of affection, you will see the value in this simple gesture. Make a mental note to look for wildflowers or make a trip to the flower stand more often. We are going to visit this idea several times in this book, but do not let that stop you from taking the initiative and doing it yourself.

For a real practical additional exercise this week, tell your partner again that you love her. Look in her eyes when you say it.

Random Fact 03

In Massachusetts it is illegal to climb into the same bed as your spouse without first having a full bath. It is rather obvious that a woman came up with this one.

Idea 4: Message on the soap

Details

You should be able to find all the requisite tools for this idea in your own home. Take a sharp knife or a toothpick, and track down a new bar of soap. Carefully carve a heart shape in the soap and put your initials in the heart, with a plus sign between them. If your name is John, for example, and your partner's name is Mary, then you would carve "J + M" into the soap. Around that masterpiece would be the heart pattern.

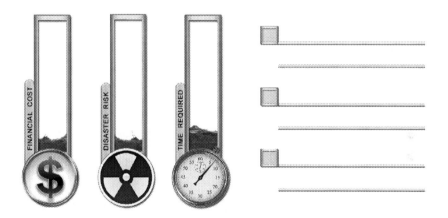

Pitfalls

If you use a sharp knife, do take care not to gash yourself and bleed all over the bathroom. Somehow the reason for the gesture might be lost. Place your "Picasso" face up in the dish or holder; she is more likely to see it that way. Furthermore, make sure that the dish isn't filled with water or soap scum. Otherwise, it is pretty hard to mess up this one. If you really want to ensure that she sees it, take a colorful piece of tissue paper and make a bed on the soap dish. Since it's not what she would normally expect to see, she undoubtedly will inspect it more closely and find your work of art.

Extras

Make a point this week to ensure that you do not stink. Shower, wash, and use deodorant. All these things are greatly appreciated by the person who shares your personal bubble. The second thing you can do is transfer the soap theme to thoughts of general cleaning. Do you ever help with or do the dishes? Why not pitch in or take over this task? It won't hurt you, will it?

Random Fact 04

Odd Labels: "Fits on head." Seen on a hotel-provided shower cap box.

Idea 5: A note in a book

Details

Let's keep it uncomplicated this week. Write "I love you, and I'm happy that you're the one I married" on a Post-it note. Place it in a book that she reads or looks at regularly. A novel or an inspirational or spiritual book is the best place to hide it. If she does crossword puzzles or peruses the *National Enquirer*, put that little note someplace among those pages. Just ensure it will be found sometime this week.

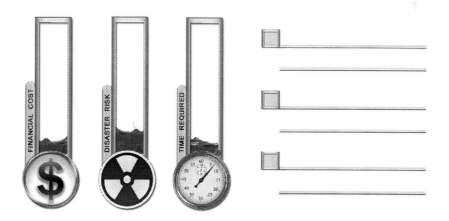

Pitfalls

If everyone in the household (other than you and your partner) uses the same book, it may get a little tricky to get her, and her alone, to read the note. If she does not read *anything* at all, then you are going to have a problem. In that situation, put it in the *TV Guide* or buy her a book—perhaps a coffee-table book with attractive photographs—and put the note in there.

Use a Post-it note and not regular paper with tape or glue. Having her tear apart her favorite book or magazine to remove your note will decrease the impact.

Extras

This week, make some other reference to your wedding, particularly its positive aspects. For some couples, their wedding day was not the best day of their lives and perhaps was even a day that they do not want to remember. (Some weddings are disasters that are best forgotten.) No matter how delightful or how dreadful that day was, however, find some aspect that was positive and brings up a happy memory. Remind your partner about that part of your wedding day and that you were thrilled to walk down the aisle with her (or to run away with her if you eloped).

> **Random Fact 05**
>
> In most advertisements, including newspapers and magazines, the time displayed on a watch or clock is 10:10. This is so the image can be mirrored without any numbers appearing backwards.

Idea 6: A note in the shower

Details

You will need a *non-permanent* felt-tip pen and someplace to write on in your shower. Since tile and paint can react negatively to the ink in markers, test a small spot first. You want to ensure that your message can be erased once it has been read.

If all goes well on that preliminary test, then write with big, bold strokes, "I love the woman standing naked in this shower!" If writing the word "naked" scares you, leave it out. If even thinking about the word causes you discomfort, use the simple "I love you" instead. However, I suspect you'll be fine because you are a man. Men are okay with the concept of naked and woman going together.

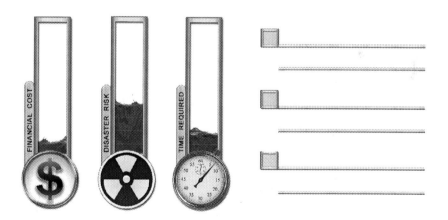

Pitfalls

If you do not test the marker, you probably will not ever be able to have guests or large parties at your home again. Or you will spend the next three nights replacing the shower. Please ensure that you can indeed expunge your little message of love and affection.

The second possible pitfall is that your partner might never see your risqué communiqué. Make sure that it is not in a direct path with the water. If she turns on the water without looking at the walls, she is likely to see nothing at all when she steps into the shower. If you need to, leave the shower curtain or shower door open.

It is probably also a good idea to make sure that your mother-in-law isn't the next one to use the shower. If she is visiting, you may want to bring flowers this week.

Extras

Your partner probably feels less than totally comfortable when she is in her natural and naked state. Most women do. It does not matter if you are married to Julia Roberts or to someone slightly less shapely. Every woman needs to feel loved, desired, and admired for how she looks, and receive regular reminders that this is the reality in which she lives. Make a point this week of reminding your partner that she is beautiful and that you only have eyes for her. Tell her that you love to look at her.

If you *do not* have eyes only for your partner, then you've got a wee bit more work to do this week ... and probably every week for the rest of your life. It is worth the struggle though, so very worth it.

Random Fact 06

According to a poll, roughly 40 percent of women have hurled footwear at a man. We do not have the stats on why, or how many hit their intended targets. Is this why some women are so into shoes? An arms race perhaps?

Idea 7: Washer and dryer love

Details

If your home is anything like mine, your partner does most (if not all) of the laundry in the home. And, in all likelihood, you will be responsible for most of the laundry being washed. Now is a good time to let her know that you appreciate all the work she does to get your stains out. Write a humble little note, something like the following:

> Darling, I sincerely appreciate all the work you do
> around the house. I appreciate that my clothes are
> clean when I need them, week after week. Thank you.

If you are a bit more squalid than most, you may want to replace the "week after week" line with "day after day." Leave the note on the washer or the dryer where she can see it next time she washes the clothes.

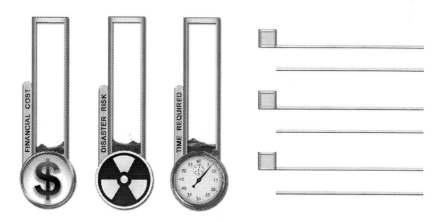

FINANCIAL COST   DISASTER RISK   TIME REQUIRED

Pitfalls

Other than falling into the washer or dryer while placing the note, it is very hard to mess this one up. Perhaps you can think of something. If you have experienced a disaster related to Idea 7, I would love to hear about it. Visit this book's website, and send me an e-mail. I'll try not to laugh.

Extras

This week, wash all your own clothes … in the kitchen sink … by hand. Actually, I am just kidding about that one. But think about what you could do to make your mate's life a little easier. For example, see to it that your dirty clothes actually make it into the hamper. Don't leave them on the floor or on the chair for her to pick up and put into the hamper for you. Think of it as a laundry three-pointer when you are down by two points, and there is less than five seconds left on the clock. Your partner will think you are even more of a superstar than if you had sunk the winning basket in the final seconds. Make this a habit.

Random Fact 07

In ancient Greece, if a woman watched even one Olympic event, she was put to death. Of course, the men competed naked, so that may have had something to do with it. Today they would just sell tickets.

26

Idea 8: A single balloon with a message

Details

This idea requires a single balloon and a felt-tip marker. In this case, it is preferable to use a pen with permanent ink rather than the one you may have earlier used in the shower.

Blow up the balloon (most men have no shortage of hot air), and tie the end firmly. Take the felt-tip pen, and write a small message for your partner on the balloon, perhaps, "I love you" or "Your love makes me feel like I could catch the wind and do just about anything." There is room for a lot of creativity here.

Once your message is complete, place the balloon somewhere in the house where she will discover it. Some examples include the bed, her breakfast plate, or the car's radio antenna.

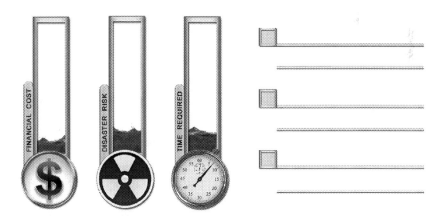

Pitfalls

Do not make the balloon look like a severed head, and then leave it lying around. Your buddies will find this very amusing, but your partner probably won't. Do not leave the balloon where very small children can find it. It would be unfortunate to have baby drool on your creation or for Junior to choke on it.

This idea can work with helium as well, but, in that case, do not inhale the helium and create a funny voice. That gag most likely wore out its welcome back in fifth grade. (I know because I tried it in sixth grade, and nobody laughed).

Extras

Balloons are all about childhood, fun, and adventure. Take some time this week to do something entertaining with your partner. It does not have to be anything wild and crazy, although that is okay too. Whatever you do, make sure it involves laughter.

Take a walk and remember a particularly humorous episode in your life together, watch a funny movie, play with the kids (if they are young enough, they will do something comical), or whatever else comes to mind. Make your partner laugh; it is one of the finest gifts you can give a person, particularly the one you chose to spend your life with.

> **Random Fact 08**
>
> The first rubber balloons were made by Professor Michael Faraday in 1824 for use in his experiments with hydrogen. He made them by pressing two circles of rubber together and letting the tacky rubber meld. Flour was used inside.

Idea 9: An e-card

Details

Most people have a computer, an Internet connection, and an e-mail address. Perhaps you and your partner share one e-mail address together (though I can't imagine why), but, either way, this idea will work.

Like a handwritten note, an e-mailed message of affection to the woman you love is sure to be well received. It does not need to be long or overly deep, but it must be sincere and from the heart. Send your partner an affectionate e-mail message today.

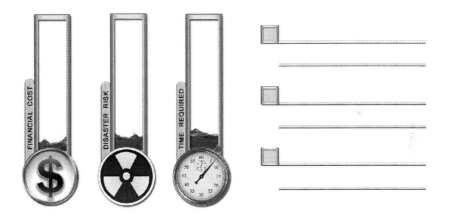

Pitfalls

Obviously, if you do not have access to a computer or an Internet connection, this idea will be a little harder to pull off. In that situation, grab your pad of Post-it notes, and leave a message for your partner somewhere in the house.

For those with computers and Internet access, the only real danger here is that someone else will read the message intended for your spouse.

Be sure that you type in that address correctly (or click the right entry in the address book), and that she checks her messages regularly. If that is done, she will have a nice surprise.

Extras

The Internet provides instant access to just about anything you can imagine. In the same way, give your partner that immediate feedback when she does things for you. A practical way to do this is to thank her every night for the dinner she prepares for you. A simple "Thanks for dinner, sweetheart, that was really good," is all it takes. Everyone likes to be appreciated, and that instant feedback will be accepted as long as it is sincere.

Random Fact 09

The average housewife walks ten miles a day around the house doing chores. If she is watching over a toddler, it is a safe bet that she could double that number easily.

Idea 10: Post-it notes all over the place

Details

It is time to up the stakes a little and bring about a greater reaction from your partner. Women like things to get grander and better, and romance (even faked romance) is no exception.

Take a stack of ten to fifteen Post-it notes, and compose a message of affection on each one. Wondering what fifteen things to say to your partner? Perhaps the list below will help you out:

1) I love you.

2) You're amazing.

3) You're beautiful.

4) I love your smile.

5) I'm so glad I married you.

6) You make my life better than I could make it on my own.

7) I thank God for you.

8) You're a wonderful mother (if she is a mother).

9) You're a great lover.

10) I love waking up each new day with you.

11) I love the times we spend together.

12) You're in my heart.

13) I love your (pick a feature, but don't be crude or mean).

14) I appreciate you.

15) Thank you for everything you do.

16) Your love means so much to me.

17) I'm so glad that we're together.

18) I want to grow old with you.

19) Be mine forever.

20) I'm yours.

Now take your messages and stick them in distinctive places around the house—on walls, doors, inside cupboards, on the mirror, on the TV, and anywhere else she might look during the day. If you place some really well, it might take several days for her to find them all.

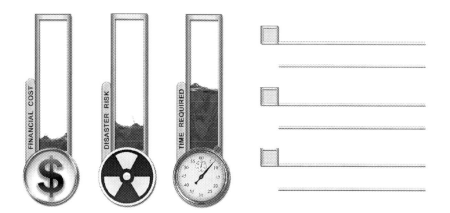

Pitfalls

If you put the wrong messages on the notes, then this idea will not work well for you. If you are unsure what to write, use the list above as a guide and save yourself some trouble and possible embarrassment. Furthermore, don't place the notes where they will never be found or where they are likely to catch fire and burn down the house (like in a burner on the stove, for example).

If you have small children, make sure that the notes are not within the reach of little hands. It is best to have your partner find them posted neatly around the house and not partially chewed and spit out on the living room carpet.

Extras

If you hide the notes adequately, so that she does not discover them all during the first day, then you have done enough. Your gift will keep on giving and surprising. If she finds them all right away, then it might be a good idea to express some of those things verbally to your partner throughout the week. Let her know she is special, loved, esteemed, appreciated, and desired. If she asks you if you mean all those things, do not tell her that you got the list out of a book and paid no attention to what you were writing. (That is a particularly bad idea.)

Idea 11: Candies in a shape on the bed

Details

Most women like some sort of candy or sweets. If you are not sure what your lifelong friend prefers (shame on you), then you will have to find out. Once you know that, this idea is very simple. Go and buy the kind she enjoys, and leave a small quantity on the bed or kitchen table. If you are able, use the candy to construct the shape of a happy face or a heart. It will make her smile and show her that you care enough about her to find her favorite indulgence and leave it as a surprise.

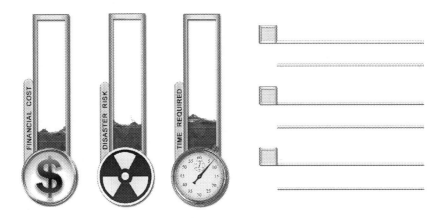

Pitfalls

If you get candy that she does not like, then you'll lose most of your intended impact. If she utterly hates the candy, you will face adversity in your relationship. If she is on a serious diet, then substitute fresh fruit or vegetable pieces instead of the candy. Nothing says "I love you" like a heart made of zucchini slices.

Once again, make sure that the dog, cat, or children do not get at the food before your partner does. If you are using zucchini, that is pretty much guaranteed. However, if you are using chocolate, security will become more of a concern.

Extras

Food and a woman's weight often go hand in hand. If your partner is sensitive about her weight (and many women are), then remind her this week that you find her exquisite and attractive. A genuine compliment can go a very long way.

If you still have a cluster of those candies left, share them with her throughout the week as well. If she finds that you gave her ten and consumed the other fifty, you may experience a rude awakening.

Random Fact 11

The estimated number of M&Ms sold each day in the United States is two hundred million. Canadians, being slightly more intelligent, prefer Smarties.

Idea 12: A store-bought
card of love or friendship

Details

Notes of adulation and affection are wonderful and certainly can have an impact in your efforts to fake the romance in your marriage. Occasionally, however, a more professional approach is required

Go to any shopping center, grocery store, card store, or corner store. Once there, make an expedition to the seldom-visited card racks. Swallowing your fear at being seen by someone you know, find a card that says "I love you" or "thinking of you." Many of these kinds of cards are available, so it should not be too hard to find one you like.

Once you have your card, compose a simple little note in it and sign it. My partner and I occasionally will underline specific words or phrases to draw attention to them. Sometimes the printed message in the card says what we want to express better than we could, so we just underline that. Whether you underline, write, or simply sign the card, the result will be equally grand. Leave it on your partner's pillow or on her breakfast or dinner plate. Do this on a random day and not her birthday, your anniversary, or any other occasion when cards are expected. It is the surprise that has the most impact.

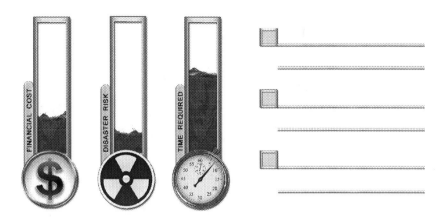

Pitfalls

Don't rely only on the picture on the front. Carefully read the card you select. Sometimes the message is not quite what you want to say. If the card says "get well soon" or "congratulations on your retirement," you might have some fast talking to do. I understand that you'll want to get away from this section of the store as speedily as possible, but do not make the mistake of bringing home a "happy anniversary" card five months before the actual date just because you admire the colors or the price.

Extras

If you are able to recover from the trauma of visiting the card aisle, you have done more than your share this week. But perhaps you could make a mental note to be aware of any difficulties your partner might be going through (real ones, not tongue-in-cheek

> **Random Fact 12**
>
> Mark Twain was born on a day in 1835 when Haley's Comet came into view. When he died in 1910, the comet came into view once again. It could certainly be argued that a bright star came and went in those years.

as referenced here), whether it is work, the kids, the in-laws, health concerns, or anything in a wide range of other possible situations. By being consciously aware and sensitive, you will make her feel special, understood, and secure.

Idea 13: A note in her date planner

Details

Hopefully, your partner has some type of system where she keeps track of all the things in her life. Most women have a wide range of things on which to keep an eye. If your partner has a date planner, then find a blank page and write "I love you" or some other note of affection. This will be something that she will see during the busy planning times, when she's trying to decide what to do or where to go next. It should put a smile on her face.

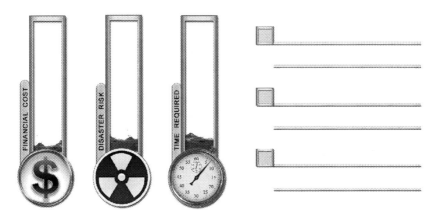

Pitfalls

If your partner uses an electronic organizer, such as those found in a Blackberry or an iPhone device, this task may be a bit harder to accomplish. You could place a small handwritten note near or on the phone. If she uses a conventional calendar, write the message on one of the days. If she does not use a calendar, date planner, or another method of keeping track, then think about getting her something for that purpose.

Extras

Most couples lead busy lives; at times, they are frantic. It is easy to face conflict in a relationship if you try to work out schedules together. This time, find a way to help your partner with her daily tasks, perhaps driving one of the kids somewhere, letting her have the car for the day, or pitching in around the house so that she has a bit of downtime. A slightly less frazzled partner is generally a happier and more responsive partner, and that can never hurt, can it?

Random Fact 13

Each year, approximately 290,000 North American husbands are attacked and physically beaten by their wives. Help stop the abuse! Buy every man a copy of this book.

Idea 14: A message on the mirror

Details

Take an erasable felt-tip marker (the erasable part is very important) and sketch a face on the bathroom mirror. Strive to be accurate about the approximate height, width, and position of your partner's head. Draw a nice smile, eyes, nose, hair, and any distinctive features. Then write the following above or beside your masterpiece: "What do you see when you look in the mirror? I see the most beautiful woman I know. I love you!"

The idea here is that she will see her own reflection within the shape you have drawn. Do not color it in, and do not make fun of your partner's features by giving her an enormous chin or Dumbo-size ears.

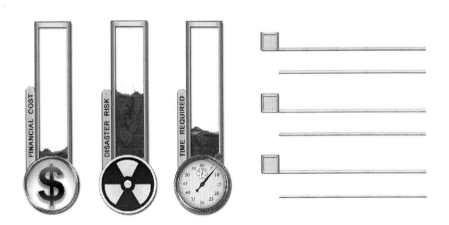

Pitfalls

The main pitfall here would be to give your partner unattractive features. This can go badly if you are unable to draw the basic shape of a head or put the eyes in the right places. This is supposed to be a romantic expression, not a Salvador Dali.

This also can go wrong if your son or father-in-law looks at the mirror. Some gender identity issues could come about from things of that nature, and you don't want to be responsible for those. In addition, do not forget how important it is to use that erasable marker. I cannot emphasize that point enough.

Extras

Once more, we are focusing on your partner's beauty (aren't women vain?), so let us make an effort to focus also on her inner allure. This week, compliment your partner on her kindness, generosity, compassion, understanding, or any of her other appealing attributes. As we know, real beauty comes from the inside. Notice your partner's lasting beauty and let her know that you have noticed it.

Fun Fact 14

Until the 1960s, men who had long hair were not permitted to enter Disneyland. Rumor has it, that in the year 2135 it will be required (as Disney buys out majority shares in the Hair Club for Men).

Idea 15: A paper card

Details

It often is the thought behind the idea that counts rather than the idea itself. To a woman, every gesture carries almost equal value. A diamond ring and a small romantic gesture carry the same weight and have close to the same impact. Diamond rings tend to be a bit more powerful than Post-it notes, but you get the idea.

Take a piece of 8.5" x 11" paper, and fold it into a small card. First, fold the top edge down to the bottom edge; then fold the left edge to the right edge. You now should have the shape of a small card with a front cover, two inside panels, and a back cover.

Now you need to be a wee bit creative and make your partner a personal card. Usually, a small image or message will go on the front. Inside, place a longer note about how much you delight in her and appreciate what she does. A verse or poem will be a nice accompaniment to your personal message.

When your card is completed, leave it where she will discover it during the day.

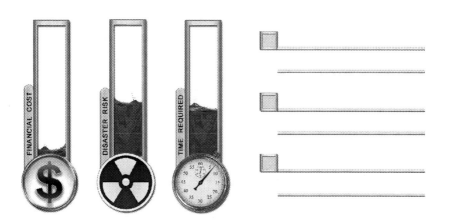

Pitfalls

If you do not know how to fold paper (despite my painfully overdone directions), draw anything, or write something meaningful, you could have difficulty with this one. Most men are not that great at crafts. (In fact, we probably use that word less than ten times in our entire lives.)

Read over the instructions for folding the paper as many times as you need to. I am confident that you will grasp that part eventually. Your toddler may be able to assist.

The card design itself is a little tougher. If you are stuck for content, you may want to cheat. Find an engaging card in the store, and copy out the short verse into your homemade card. Do not copy it in the store itself, and do not give your partner that precise card later either. If images are hard to come up with, try a simple heart or just use words and add a little color. There's nothing to it.

Extras

Verses and poems are like music and can have the same impact. If your house is anything like mine, odds are your partner and you have different tastes in music. Sometime this week, make a point of playing the music that she likes and not the stuff that you like. (If your musical interests are the same, then this will be easy).

Again, it is the small gestures that show you care enough about her to put her first. That certainly is as powerful as a diamond (at least a small one).

Idea 16: A note on the pillow

Details

Many of the ideas that we have executed so far have focused on starting your partner's day off the right way. It is always wonderful to start the day with a thought and impression of being loved. It is also a great way to conclude the day, and that is what is behind this next plan. All you need to do is write "I love you" in some memorable way. Since you are going to sleep, perhaps it would be nice to write, "Honey, at the end of every day, I'm so thankful that I've had you in my life today and that I'm ending the day with you."

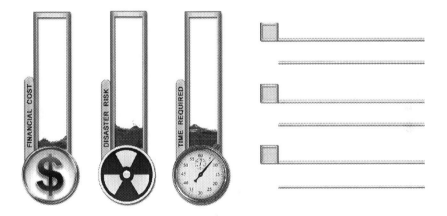

Pitfalls

Some women throw back the covers with a vengeance. If that is the case in your house, your note may go soaring into the air, never to be seen again. A tiny piece of tape will ensure that your message is seen rather than lost in the shuffle. The best thing to do is place the note on your partner's pillow.

If your partner goes to bed very late and is unlikely to read your message, wait for another opportunity that seems more appropriate.

Extras

There is one infallible way to start and end every day on the right foot. Always tell your partner you love her, and give her a kiss. Do this both in the morning before you leave the house and in the evening before you go to sleep. If those are the last words you say before you drift off, then there can never be any regrets as you commence the next day. And suppose those were your final words on this earth? Can you think of any more apt?

Fun Fact 16

Isaac Asimov is the only author to have a book published in every Dewey Decimal category. He wrote over 500 books in his lifetime. Approximately 495 of those are worth reading.

Idea 17: A favorite magazine

Details

Reading is good for the mind and the soul. Think about how beneficial reading this book has been for you! There is nothing like a high-quality book to stimulate and entertain. Sometimes, however, you have neither the time nor the energy for a full book. In that instance, a magazine may fit the bill. Most people have particular interests that are the focus of one or another magazine. Perhaps your partner already has a favorite. Go to the store, pick up the latest issue, and invite her to take a break with it.

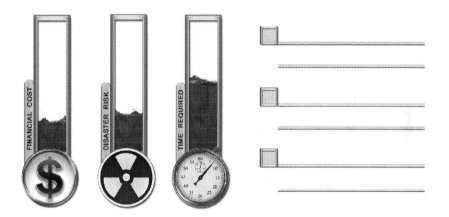

Pitfalls

Resist the urge to buy your partner a magazine on a topic that you think she should appreciate. If you surprise her with the latest issue of *Guns and Ammo*, you may not get the charitable thanks that we are "shooting" for here. Remember, this gift is for her. Similarly, if you bring a magazine on weight-loss tips, you may find yourself sleeping on the couch for a week.

Try not to carry home anything for yourself. Your gift will have a lot less impact if she sees you reading something new as well. It will be a great deal more impressive if you went to the store with the sole purpose of finding her something wonderful.

Do not linger by the skin magazines either; that is not the best way to show your affection and devotion toward your lover.

Extras

Now that she has a great magazine, she'll need some time to read it. The best way you can ensure that she has some leisure time is to help out with the housework. If you shoo her off after dinner to read your gift while you do the supper dishes, you will get a lot of mileage from this gesture. Maybe washing dishes is not the best thing you can do to help your partner, but odds are you'll know what is (if you give it some thought). Find something, and do it for her. It will speak volumes.

> **Fun Fact 17**
>
> Mozart wrote twelve variations on the nursery rhyme, "Twinkle, Twinkle, Little Star" at the age of twenty-five. Did we really need that many versions?

Idea 18: Little notes in a magazine

Details

Remember the magazine you bought for your partner? Is it still around somewhere? Find it or whatever publication she is currently reading. Take a Post-it note (or several), and write "I love you" on it. Find a few random spots in the pages of the book, and hide the message(s) there. Next time your partner picks up the issue and flips through it, your notes will be sure to bring a smile to her face.

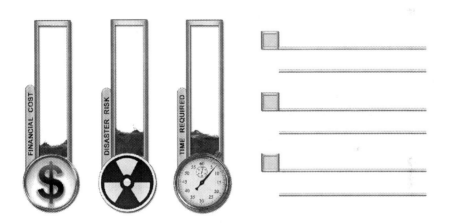

Pitfalls

If other family members are likely to read the magazine with your notes, be mindful about what you place on them. If your partner is not reading the issue that you selected, your efforts will be wasted. Sometimes it can take a while before your notes are found, but that is fine. As long as the magazine is browsed within the next several days, you will be in good shape.

When I first tried this with my partner, I had to wait almost a week and a half before she eventually opened and read the magazine. I kept placing it in what I thought were obvious spots, hoping she would get the hint and pick the darn thing up. Eventually she did, and all my blatant hints finally became clear. It made her laugh, and that was its own reward.

Extras

If she is excited about the magazine—whether it is the one you bought her last week or another one—consider subscribing to it for her. If she already has a subscription (or you are not financially able to purchase one at this point), make a mental note to pick up an issue for her now and then.

Remember also that your partner will once again need time and opportunity to peruse what she has in front of her. Enough said.

Fun Fact 18

In Texas, it is illegal to put graffiti on someone else's cow. Painting your own livestock with gang symbols is apparently okay. There is no word on where the horses stand in all this.

Idea 19: A message
on the toilet paper roll

Details

This idea is a little off the beaten path, and it requires your companion to have at least some sense of humor. Generally, the bathroom is not the place where most people reflect upon romance, but why not have a little amusement?

Take a felt-tip marker, and draw a heart or smiley face on one of the first squares of toilet paper on the roll. The idea here is for your partner to reach for the roll and see your message or sketch. If she is a little light-hearted, it should make her smile despite the compromised position she'll be in when she reads it.

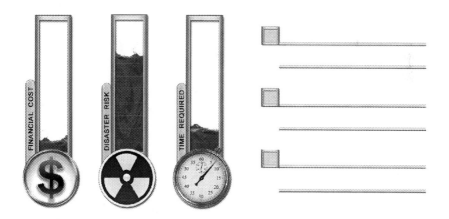

Pitfalls

I have to admit, there are a few more pitfalls with this idea than with many of the others, but sometimes a bit of peril is worth it. Here are a few of the potential complications: If your partner has absolutely no sense of humor, she may get annoyed with you for wasting a few sheets of toilet paper. If she uses the paper before she sees the artwork, then your endeavors will have been for nothing. If you use a permanent marker and some ink remains on her skin, well, let's not go there, okay? Most significant, make no reference to the reason she may be sitting there. No good can come of it. Be undaunted but wise, and give this one a shot.

Extras

Men tend to spend a lot more time in the bathroom than women do. Next time you are in there, take a quick look around. Is the towel on the rack, is the soap in the dish, is the sink rinsed, and (double-check this!) is the toilet seat down? It is the little things that can grate on the nerves and make a big difference in your marriage. If it vexes her, make an effort to address it.

If men can assemble a rocket and go to the moon, we certainly can drop the seat and keep the peace, no matter how illogical it may seem.

Fun Fact 19

When the Scott Paper Company first began manufacturing toilet paper, they did not put their name on the packaging because of embarrassment. It no longer seems to be a problem for them.

Idea 20: A message in a bottle

Details

You are at Idea 20 already! See how well you are doing? It is time to up the ante a bit and pull out all the stops. Do not fear, though; this idea is not as hard as you might think.

The message in a bottle idea hails back to those old stories in which a person stranded on a deserted island put a message in a bottle for his loved ones and tossed it into the ocean. The hope was that relatives would someday find the message and realize how much they were loved.

You do not have to get stranded on an island to do this, though. All you need to do is find a stylish bottle with a cork, available in department stores everywhere. You will also need some nice paper, perhaps something that resembles parchment.

Write a nice message on the paper, either your own creation or one copied from a store-bought greeting card. Sign and date your message. Then roll the paper up, slide it into the bottle, and pop in the cork.

Leave it somewhere for your sweetheart to find.

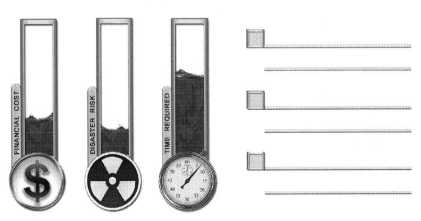

Pitfalls

When shopping for a bottle, make sure that your paper will fit into it. Nothing is quite as frustrating as trying to cram an 8.5" piece of paper into a 5" bottle. Find a bottle with a wide enough mouth so that the paper will be able to come out again. Roll it up tightly, and then fasten a small piece of ribbon or tape around it so that it can slide out easily. Try it a few times first to make sure it works.

You may not be able to find the perfect empty bottle. I ended up buying some unusual Asian cooking sauce and pouring it down the drain, just to get the bottle I wanted. A wash and a rinse, and it was all good to go. I am sure your mother told you not to waste, but sometimes love requires sacrifice.

If this is done right, then your partner will keep the bottle and message somewhere to remind herself how wonderful you are. Now, wouldn't that be nice?

Extras

If you do this right, there will be thanks enough. I will not burden you with anything else. Just live the message of love that you placed in the bottle with your words, actions, and thoughts. Remind yourself this week what it would be like to be separated from the one you love without ever knowing if you are going to see her again. It is amazing how much that can change your attitude and feelings toward someone.

Fun Fact 20

Coconuts kill more people each year than sharks or tigers. Approximately 150 people are slain by coconuts yearly. Sharks are responsible for the deaths of roughly five people a year. Tigers kill close to 100 people a year.

Idea 21: A heart on a sandwich

Details

Without even knowing your partner at all, I'll wager that she eats sandwiches on occasion. (I'm sure you are saying, how does he do it?) Your mission this week is to make the commonplace daily food routine more romantic. This is not as involved as it sounds. All you need to do is find a way to make a heart shape somewhere on the piece of cuisine that *you* are going to prepare for her. If you are making anything with sauce or spread, this should be relatively uncomplicated. For example, make a peanut butter and jelly sandwich, and use a toothpick or a knife to draw a heart shape in the spread. Serve it open-faced. Mission accomplished.

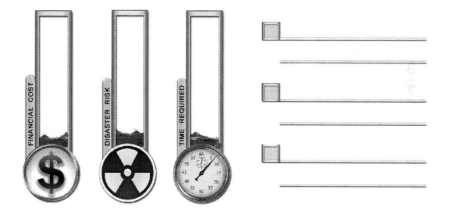

Pitfalls

Your partner may not like bread or peanut butter. The thought of food may lead to all sorts of negativity if she is on a severe diet. In that situation, construct a heart or smiley face using cucumber or carrot slices.

Use a little imagination, and you'll find a way to give her something tasty in a manner that brings a smile to her face.

Extras

Food preparation is labor intensive. Sometime this week, give your partner a respite and take her out to dinner or order in something. Even a quick meal out will be appreciated after a long and hectic day. No preparation. No dishes. No worries. It is worth the negligible expense to show her you love her in this way. This idea is particularly effective if it comes from you. She works hard, and you suggest that she not cook. How can it fail?

Fun Fact 21

Baskin-Robbins once made ketchup ice cream. After all, kids like ketchup on just about everything right? Sadly, it was a complete failure. Word has it that the recipe was purchased by Hostess. All seems to have worked out okay there.

Idea 22: A gift certificate
for a night out with friends

Details

If you are like most couples with children (especially young ones), it can be complicated to find the time to get out and see friends. Women need the companionship of other women and a break from the youngsters (and, occasionally, their husbands).

This idea requires a regular 8.5" x 11" piece of paper. Place it in front of you and fold it down into two or three equal-sized pieces. Cut off one of the pieces with scissors and write on it, in large, bold letters, "GIFT CERTIFICATE." Below that, write "Redeem for a night out with friends. Babysitting provided."

Then put the certificate in a sealed envelope, and give it to her at an appropriate time.

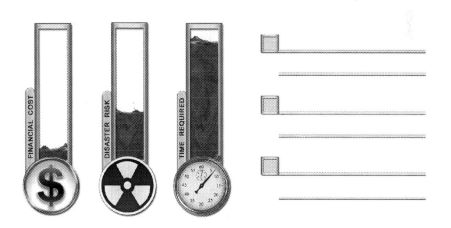

Pitfalls

Planning a night out with friends can take some doing. Do not expect her to redeem this immediately, and be prepared for this to come up weeks or even months later. The pitfall for you would be to grumble about staying at home with the kids while she is out with her friends. Your schedule and plans will have to take a back seat. If you are gracious in the giving, take a similar approach in the redeeming. In most cases, it is unlikely that your partner will plan her night out for the evening that you will play the deciding game in the finals, so do not fret too much. Just remember to be gracious when the time comes.

Extras

Win that final game. Every woman loves a hero, as long as he does not leave his sweaty gear in the middle of the living room floor. If you are accommodating and agreeable when you give her the certificate, you will earn your stripes. How could she request anymore of you?

Fun Fact 22

A Quebec junior hockey player from the 1930s was hit by a puck during a game. The impact ignited a set of matches he had in his pocket. His uniform caught fire, and he suffered serious burns before the fire could be put out.

Idea 23: An exotic postcard

Details

Most of us would love to travel but do not often get the chance. That does not mean that we cannot dream and plan and have a little fun with the thought of getting away. I'm sure you and your partner have spent at least a little time talking about the places that you would like to visit someday.

In the meantime, make each day with your spouse an adventure. Send her a postcard, and tell her that every day with her is like a vacation. (Yes, even if it's not.) For some added fun, include a variation on the "the weather is beautiful, wish you were here" theme, perhaps: "the weather is beautiful, glad you are here" or "the weather sucks, sure glad you're here."

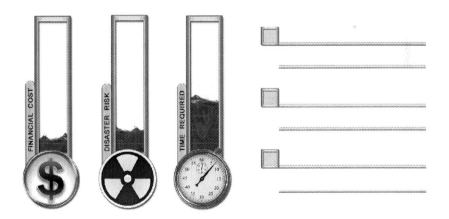

Pitfalls

Unless you forget your own address or are unable to stick a stamp on an envelope, this idea is pretty hard to mess up.

Pick a respectable postcard with an appropriate photo on the front. The one with the girls in thongs may seem attractive to you, but your partner neither will post it on the fridge nor reward you for your thoughtfulness.

Extras

You may not be able to get on a plane and fly away, but nothing should stop you from taking a local day trip. Pack a lunch or plan on eating out, and locate a nice place to have a "holiday" for the day. Virtually every location in the world has some interesting and intriguing places nearby. If you cannot think of anywhere to go, have a picnic in the backyard or the living room. A respite can be had just about anywhere.

Fun Fact 23

Ingrown toenails are hereditary, along with dimpled cheeks, the ability to roll your tongue, and type of earlobes. Just one more thing to thank your loving parents for.

Idea 24: A Post-it note in the newspaper

Details

If you subscribe to a local or national newspaper, surprise her with a little love note somewhere among the pages. Use one of your trusty Post-it notes, or take a dark pen and write on the paper itself. All it takes is "I love you" (or something similar), and your effort will be a triumphant success.

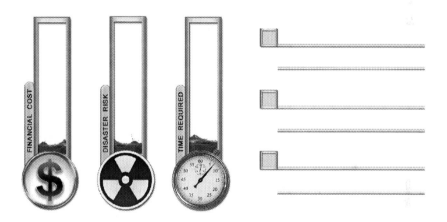

Pitfalls

For this to work, you have to get to the paper before she does. I recommend preparing your note ahead of time, so that a quick and covert insertion is possible, if required.

If you use a felt-tip marker or a pen to write your message on the paper itself, avoid writing over anything that she may want to read.

Extras

Why settle for only one note? See how many you can conceal among the pages of a book, magazine, or newspaper. If one works well, more will work better, right? Suppose every page of the paper had a message for her, or the complete note was in parts so she could put it together slowly? News about local roadwork delays never will be so memorable.

Fun Fact 24

The IRS employees' tax manual has instructions for collecting taxes after a nuclear war. Seems like both death and taxes really are inevitable.

Idea 25: A rose on the pillow

Details

As mentioned earlier, a single flower can have a commanding impact. Over the ages, the flower has been a strong representation of love and romance. The rose is especially associated with this emotion. This week, buy (or take from a neighbor's garden in the dead of night) a single long-stemmed red rose. Leave the rose on your partner's pillow so that she will find it when she prepares for bed.

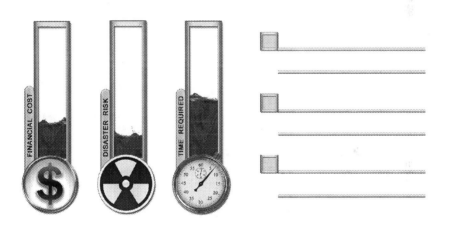

Pitfalls

Hiding the rose before you are ready to put it on the bed at night might be difficult. The greatest impact will come from the surprise factor. Seeing you walk into the house with a rose is nice, but being surprised with it later is much nicer. Locate a cool spot—in the garage, for example—that can serve as a good hiding place. Do not put it under tools or leave it lying in plain sight, and you should be able to pull this off.

Extras

Think about what else you can accomplish for your partner in the bedroom. Are any of your clothes on the floor? Is the bed made? Is there a pile of junk on your dresser? (There always seems to be one on mine.)

Look for other ways to make your bedroom a great place. It is the room where you rest, love, and refresh, so try to make the atmosphere reflect that theme.

Fun Fact 25

Columbus's crew picked a rose branch out of the ocean on October 11, 1492. This signaled the presence of land. The very next day, Columbus discovered America.

Idea 26: A snail-mail card

You probably are well acquainted with the card aisle at the store by now, since we've spent over a year working on these ideas. Now you are going to take one further step in your education and revisit the place to find another card for your partner.

Think about the cards that you have used so far, and choose one with a slightly different theme. If you have chosen "I love you" cards in the past, look at some that focus on friendship or have a "just for fun" theme. If your partner is going through a hardship (connected to the kids, work, friends, or your marriage), a "thinking of you" card is a good choice.

Once you have located your card and either have written a little note or have underlined the key words and phrases that communicate your message, you are ready for the final step. Put the card in the envelope, write your own address on the front, put a stamp on it, and drop it in the mail. It will be a pleasant surprise for her in a few days.

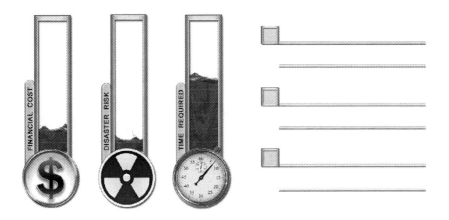

Pitfalls

If you do not know your own mailing address, this might not be for you. Sometimes I copy the address from a piece of mail that someone else has sent to me. It works every time. You might have to beg, borrow, or steal a stamp from someone you know. It is really quite hard to mess this idea up, though, isn't it?

Extras

What else could you put in that envelope? Maybe a bookmark with a verse or poem, a gift certificate, some other interesting item —use your imagination. Even something small, like ten-dollar gift certificate to Starbucks (which may be enough to buy her an empty cup), probably would be appreciated. Think about what your partner will appreciate the most. I know a fellow who put a condom in the card, as a hint. It was an ill-conceived idea.

> **Fun Fact 26**
>
> On the cartoon show *The Jetsons*, Jane Jetson is thirty-three years old. Her daughter Judy is fifteen. That means her husband, George, would be charged with a criminal offense in most of the world. Maybe law is different in the future.

Idea 27: Balloon bouquet

Details

With luck, the single balloon idea was a success, and the flowers have been doing the trick as well. Why not combine the two? I am not suggesting that you give her balloons and roses at the same time (thorns and latex do not mix well), but to design a bouquet of balloons.

Go to any store that sells balloons. A specialty store will be your best bet, but any place that carries balloons will do. Look for twelve red balloons that will not be much larger than a softball when they are blown up. The balloons should be blank.

Also purchase twelve plastic stems; most balloon stores will have them on hand. Blow up the balloons, and secure them to the sticks. Get them wrapped up similar to a flower bouquet, and take them home to your partner. If she has a sense of fun, she will love this idea.

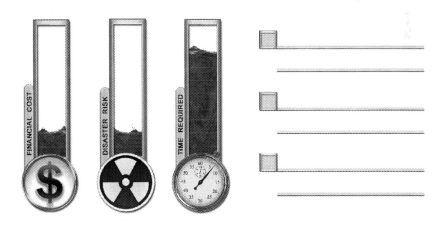

FINANCIAL COST   DISASTER RISK   TIME REQUIRED

Pitfalls

If the balloons have any printing on them, they will not look nearly as good. It is not a great idea to present twelve McDonald's balloons to your partner in a bouquet. Also resist the urge to fashion the stems yourself. Balloon stores sell little plastic stems that ensure that the balloon sits on the top (like a flower) and does not hang limply off to the side—that might send the wrong message.

Extras

If you want to really have an impact, take a felt-tip marker and write a small message on each balloon. "I love you," "you are amazing," "best friend," among other phrases, will work well. Take a look at Idea 10 for a list of appropriate phrases of love and affection. Of course, you may want to do this without messages the first time and with messages another time.

I can testify that this idea was one of the most memorable of all the things I have ever put together for my partner.

Fun Fact 27

There are more recreational golfers per capita in Canada than in any other country in the world. I guess it's not all igloos and dogsleds then. But after winter 2010, everyone knows that, right?

Idea 28: A note on your kid's food

Details

If you are doing this in order, then the brilliant balloon bouquet of the past few weeks should still be on display, bringing a smile to your partner's face every day. We do not want to overdo it and perhaps become a real romantic (rather than just fake it really well). This week, we'll employ something a little lower key.

Take a Post-it note, and write a brief message to your spouse, thanking her for the food she prepares for you and the kids. Place it on the children's cereal box or something else that she prepares for the family.

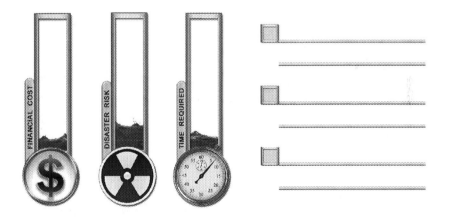

Pitfalls

Place the Post-it note on something that she's bound to see in the morning. Make sure that the message is encouraging and will start her day off right. Writing "thanks for finally making a decent meal yesterday" does not provide an optimistic beginning to her day. And it won't do anything for your day either; trust me on that one.

Extras

Help her with some of the food preparation. Help her feed the kids in the morning or on the weekend. Does any of this sound like it might boost your points with her a little? (Not that I advocate keeping a points system, as it is generally a poor idea.)

Feeding the kids on weekend mornings gives my wife a break. Saturday mornings are a great time for me to cook bacon, eggs, and waffles for the family, always with the kids' "assistance." Find a way to provide a little extra support in the kitchen this week.

Fun Fact 28

The United States has never lost a war in which donkeys were used. However, there has been at least one ass in every conflict in the world's history. If there were none, wars would never start.

Idea 29: A massage

Details

Typically when men think about massage, they imagine a woman (hopefully, a loved one) rubbing their back (ahem!) and easing the tension of a hard day. But if you don't recognize that your partner has days on which a massage might be the medication called for, then you are missing the boat.

Offer to give your partner a therapeutic neck and back massage. Resist the inclination to turn it into a seduction, and just serve her selflessly. There are very few women who will not relish this kind of attention.

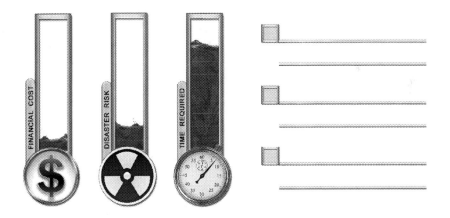

Pitfalls

The massage has to last for more than five minutes to have an impact. I suggest that twenty minutes or more be the minimum. If your hands start to hurt, then alternate between a softer and a deeper rub, but keep at it and without complaint.

Do not massage so hard that you hurt her. The idea is to relax and refresh, not mold like a piece of silly putty. Observe her body language, and you will know what she desires.

Extras

Some women love to have their feet rubbed (my partner actually detests it). If your partner likes it, then move down from the back and shoulders and go to work on her feet too. Or find something else that can be pleasurable. My partner loves to have her scalp massaged (if you've never tried this, you should; it is great), and so that is what I do for her. I am confident that you'll discover the next logical step.

If she is really tense, experiment with some hot massage oil. It can work wonders.

Fun Fact 29

Tablecloths were originally meant to serve as towels with which guests could wipe their hands and faces after dinner.

Idea 30: A note on the bathroom door

Details

We are going to get as much mileage out of a small pack of Post-it notes as we can. There are literally hundreds of ways to utilize them, and I will do my best to uncover what they all are.

This time, we are going to venture into the bathroom again. Compose a brief note on a Post-it and place it on the back of the bathroom door. Write anything at all; just make sure it is positive. "I love you" is fine and has a continued celebrated effect as everyone needs to be reminded often of his or her partner's affection and dedication.

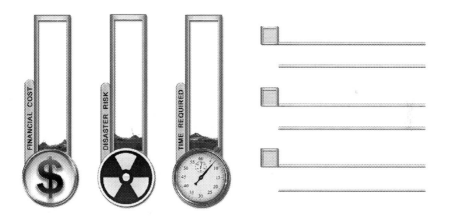

Pitfalls

If she never closes the bathroom door, then she may never see your note. If your teenage daughter uses the bathroom first, you may have some embarrassment added to your life. Being slightly aware of your partner's morning or evening schedule and planning accordingly should help you avoid these minefields. If you have a private bathroom off the master bedroom, then you are set and cannot fail.

Extras

Save some water this week and shower with your partner. Wash her back for her. (This is not going to be *all* hard work.) There is really nothing quite as glorious as embracing under a stream of hot water and feeling it run over the two of you together. (Well, I lie. There are slightly better things, but this is a seriously marvelous start.)

Fun Fact 30

Winston Churchill was born in a ladies' room during a dance. Not everything associated with dancing is evil.

Idea 31: A snail-mail letter

Details

Electronic communication has almost totally eliminated the use of postal mail for quick notes and greetings. Most of us probably still mail Christmas cards and the odd bill, but e-mail is so much more effective when you want to send a quick line or two.

Despite this, the joy of receiving a letter has not been lost and, in fact, may have grown as a result. Since people seldom receive letters anymore, they are more unique and memorable. This week, do the unusual, and write your partner a letter.

Your letter should have a decent amount of material and be both meaningful and heartfelt. Tell her how much you fancy her. Point out things you've appreciated about her over the past several weeks. Remind her about some great recollection the two of you share.

Then plop it in an envelope, and mail it.

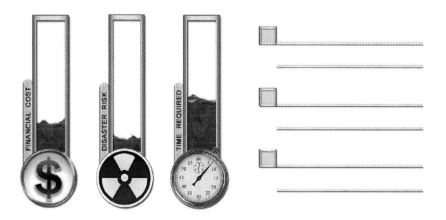

Pitfalls

Since presumably you already have sent a card via mail, you should know your own address by now.

If your handwriting is anything like mine, you may want to type your letter instead of write it. I occasionally write and mail myself a letter because the mystery of trying to decipher what I said gives me great amusement. For your partner, however, aim for legibility rather than mystery.

Extras

If you want to, you can include a small token in the envelope, such as a bookmark, gift certificate, or coupon for something particular. If you want to do something different, then for a bonus and some real impact, write your letter in rhyme (or borrow a verse from Shakespeare or T. S. Eliot). A love poem in the mail is guaranteed to get a reaction.

Fun Fact 31

Daddy longlegs (cellar spiders) are thought to be more poisonous than black widow spiders, but simply can't bite a human due to their jaws or short teeth. However, this is a myth; daddy longlegs can bite and they are not poisonous.

Idea 32: Coffee or tea delivery

Details

Straightforward things have the greatest impact. Acts of service, in contrast to a "serve me" attitude, make a marriage strong and lasting. Acts of service do not have to be big to make a memorable impression; something as small as serving your partner a drink will do.

If your partner enjoys coffee or tea, find an appropriate time to make her a cup. This means that you will make *all* the preparations; getting her a refill from a pot of coffee that she made will not cut it. Take the little time it will necessitate and bring her a fresh cup. If she's a fan of a particular type of tea or something more exotic than pedestrian coffee, make that your mission.

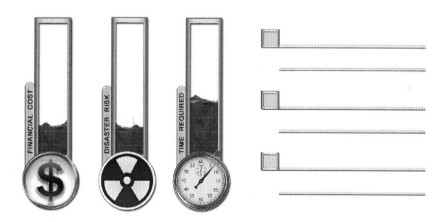

Pitfalls

If she already has consumed five or six cups of coffee, she may not be in the mood for another cup. Gauge the situation well and pick an appropriate time. Perhaps offer her that first cup in the morning or that final one in the evening.

If your partner drinks neither coffee nor tea, then you have more of a challenge on your hands. There is always hot chocolate, or you can take her a cold soft drink or glass of water.

Extras

Along with the coffee or tea, pick up a special flavor of the beverage as a surprise. A gourmet coffee or a new herbal tea may be received with great appreciation.

For additional extra credit this week, have a quiet talk with your partner while you enjoy the fruits of your labor. At night, my partner and I often share a hot cup of tea, dim the lights, put on some soft music, and perhaps light a few candles. Then we talk to each other quietly, about anything in our hearts. It always turns into a delightful time of sharing and connecting. This is particularly effective if you have a difficult matter to discuss. Lowered lights often mean lowered voices, which can mean calmer emotions. Things sort themselves out a great deal more amicably in that type of environment.

Fun Fact 32

Levi Strauss didn't call them jeans. He called them "waist overalls." Marketing quickly stepped in and changed that. Thank you, marketing.

Idea 33: Bubble bath or shower gel

Details

I assume that your partner takes either a shower or a bath regularly. If she does not, then please do not invite me over for tea during the summer months.

Your mission, should you choose to accept it, is to make a small expedition to a local drug or specialty store that sells women's health and beauty products. Buy her some refreshing and rejuvenating bath or shower gel. If you find one that moistens and softens the skin, chances are she will appreciate it greatly.

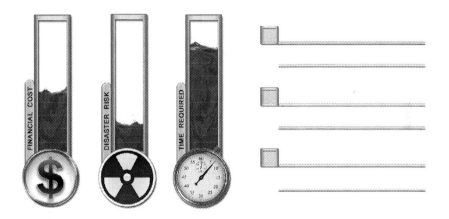

Pitfalls

Feeling like you will be out of your element in a bath and beauty store? Well, you in all likelihood will be, but that is why stores have friendly and obliging sales assistants—for people like you and me. Each Christmas I go to The Body Shop and find a few stocking stuffers for my partner. The experience is seldom painful. If it is your first time, just take a deep breath, gather your courage, and stride in confidently. The sales assistants are trained to smell terror so do not let it show!

When investing in something for your partner, make sure the product will not cause an allergic reaction or an infection. Here, again, the sales staff will be of help.

Extras

Your partner is going to need the time to enjoy her new gift, so what do you think your extra should be? No, really—guess! If I have to explain it to you, then you are beyond my help. And I'm not giving any hints either.

Fun Fact 33

During WW2, because many players were called to serve, the Pittsburgh Steelers and the Philadelphia Eagles combined to become the Steagles.

Idea 34: A note on the car

Details

If your partner drives, then this idea is a very straightforward one, and unlikely to cause any inconvenience for you. Leave a note for her on the steering wheel so she will discover it the next time she drives the car.

Use a Post-it note or another small piece of paper and write "I love you," or some other simple message, and leave it for her to discover. If you can be more creative, that will be worth some additional smiles and have a greater impact.

One idea I have used is to draw small Scrabble-like squares and write the "I love" words going across and the "you" coming down and sharing the "o" with the word "love." Then I add tile points to the corners of the squares, and voila! It was something unsophisticated and different, but it worked.

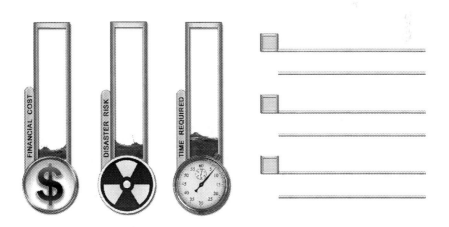

Pitfalls

Your partner may not be partial to Scrabble. She may not drive very often. You may have trouble writing neatly or drawing little squares. There are doubtless books on each of these topics that can assist you. Leave the note elsewhere if your partner is not likely to take the car. Draw a picture if she cannot read and bypass the Scrabble idea if the squares challenge you.

Other than these potentially serious obstacles, this idea is quite foolproof.

Extras

Give your partner a reason to take the car out. Perhaps an afternoon or an evening trip to see a friend is in order. She might want to run some errands, perhaps without the kids, if there are any at home, and you could make that possible for her.

One other possible way to earn some extra credit this week is to make sure the car is clean, particularly if she has her own vehicle. A wash and a clean will be immensely appreciated. If you share a family vehicle, make sure it is washed, cleaned, and perhaps has a new air freshener hanging from the mirror when she drives away.

> **Fun Fact 34**
>
> In the last four thousand years, no new animals have been domesticated. This includes *Hormonus-Extremitus*, commonly known as the teenager.

Idea 35: A children's book

Details

A children's storybook often embodies the emotion and straightforward thoughts that adults want to convey. Using unique imagery, these books are designed to seize the imagination and wonder of a child. Occasionally, a book comes along that resonates with adults as well. This time you are going to track down a specific book and give it to your partner—a love letter in a book format.

The book in question is called *Guess How Much I Love You*, written by Sam McBratney and illustrated by Anita Jeram. It narrates the story of two hares who tell each other how much they delight in one another. It is a wonderfully illustrated and brilliant book.

The book is available on thick card stock (the kind that little babies chew on) and also as a regular hardcover and paperback. It is published by Candlewick Press and should be obtainable from most bookstores and certainly via Amazon.com and other online bookstores.

Find the book. Write a brief notation inside for your loved one, and you will create a lasting memory.

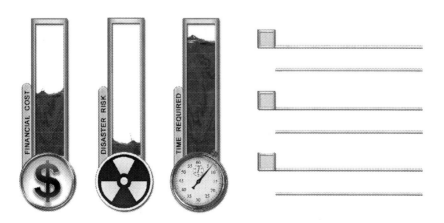

Pitfalls

It may take a bit of time to track down this book if your local bookstore does not have it. Be diligent and patient, and you will be able to smoke it out. If it takes some effort to locate and have it shipped to you, consider it an exercise in the wonders of online ordering and patience.

Certainly other books will convey this same message to your loved one, but I strongly recommend this one and encourage you to find it.

Extras

Be sure to write in the front of the book before giving it to your mate This is a present that should not end up on the shelf with the other children's books but should be on her dresser, desk, or other place where she can look at it and remember your affection.

Fun Fact 35

This year, more than 2.5 million books will be shipped with the wrong covers. I apologize if you thought you were getting an Italian cookbook.

Idea 36: Hidden candy

Details

Almost everyone has a sweet tooth. In an earlier step, we went over the necessity of finding out what your partner likes to eat. Hopefully, you still possess that information.

Purchase a bag of her favorite candy or chocolates and hide them all around the house so she can uncover them throughout the day, possibly even the week following, depending on how well you conceal them. The notion here is to present a sweet surprise to your partner that she will discover when she opens cupboard doors, pulls out her makeup kit, or walks to the washing machine.

If you hide around twenty-five to thirty pieces of candy, you should achieve the maximum effect.

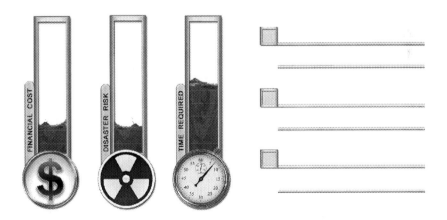

Pitfalls

If your partner is on a diet, you may not come across as overly supportive. Hide something like grapes instead, but if they are not found right away—yetch. There are several low-fat or low-sugar sweets that can be used as an alternative, including various all-natural choices. You may have to hunt a little, but some stores will stock them.

If you have small children or teenagers in the house, it will be challenging to get them to leave these delicacies alone. Perhaps bring them in on the plan and give them the remaining candies in the bag in exchange for leaving your hidden stashes in place.

Pets are less likely to come to a similar agreement with you, so plan accordingly. It is not very romantic for your partner to come upon the dog vomiting up chocolate on the living room carpet.

Extras

You can find very petite pads of Post-it notes. Perhaps a tiny note with each treat would increase the impact.

Throughout the week, make an effort to convey appreciation for her "sweet" points. Encourage her with comments that show you notice and value her warmth, humor, understanding, compassion, hard work, faithfulness, etc.

Verbally encouraging her will leave an even longer-lasting memory than the sweets, and it's fat-free.

Fun Fact 36

Denmark has the highest per capita consumption of candy in the world, at 29.5 pounds per person annually.

Idea 37: A flower bouquet

Details

Hopefully, this concept requires little explanation. Most men have, at one time or another, brought home flowers for their wives. In many cases, this occurs only on Valentine's Day or an anniversary. Flowers invariably have the greatest impact when they are just because you love her. If you are moving through this book in order, you are already a seasoned individual in horticultural gift giving.

Trek to the flower store, select a nice seasonal bouquet, have it wrapped, take it home. Simple, isn't it? It makes you wonder why men don't do this more often (perhaps because flowers cost so much!).

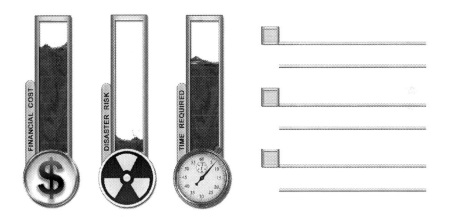

Pitfalls

You cannot persuade me that your partner does not take pleasure in flowers, not even a little. You cannot tell me that you are powerless to locate a place that sells flowers. You cannot honestly expect me to believe that you have no inkling about how to purchase flowers. That pretty much takes care of all the possible cop-outs; there really is no significant danger or pitfall associated with this idea.

Place the flowers and some water in a vase that is size-appropriate (so it does not tip over and make a huge mess), and this task is concluded.

Extras

Obtain some of that plant "food stuff" when you buy the flowers. It is always agreeable when the blossoms last for more than a day.

Look outside at your own yard (I apologize to those living in apartments) and see if anything needs doing. Even in winter, there is typically something to clean up, organize, or beautify. See what you can find to make your home a bit more appealing.

If your spouse has been nagging you to mow the lawn or weed the garden, consider starting there.

Fun Fact 37

If you toss a penny 10,000 times, it will not be heads 5,000 times, but more like 4,950. The heads' picture weighs slightly more, so it ends up on the bottom more often.

Idea 38: Chalk on the driveway

Details

This idea is somewhat seasonal. If your driveway is covered in snow, or you are in the middle of a very rainy season, revisit this scheme in the warmer months.

It requires some sidewalk chalk. If you have small children, there is a good probability you have some of this at hand. If not, a dollar store can sell you a box. On your driveway, in your carport, on the sidewalk, or somewhere else appropriate, draw a large heart and put your and your partner's names inside of it. Draw an arrow through it if you are feeling particularly artistic. Leave it for her (or the kids) to find.

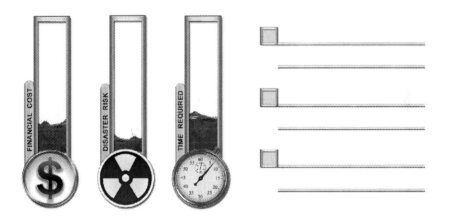

Pitfalls

Ensure that the surface you are drawing on will wash clean. Most road or driveway surfaces will not present any problem, but it is always a good idea to test a small area first.

Do not park the car over your masterpiece. My bride seldom crawls under the car to look for hidden messages and, unless your partner is different than most, she will drive over your gesture.

Do not leave the chalk out if there are problem teenagers nearby. Your message may have been altered substantially by the time your partner sees it.

Extras

A man's garage frequently can be his private domain. If he possesses a workshop, then there is a high chance that his partner has never seen the inside of it and is not permitted to wander in without permission. Everyone requires his or her own space in which to do hobbies or find some quiet time.

For the extra effort, do one of two things: 1) If your partner routinely walks into your garage or workshop, and it is a disaster area, you could clean it up a bit. 2) If your domain is sacred, or just immaculate, then look for ways to ensure your partner has her own space and an opportunity to enjoy it.

This is not always feasible and may take some creative brainstorming on your part. I am confident that you are up to the enterprise.

Fun Fact 38

The average North American will eat 35,000 cookies during their lifetime. At least 7,200 of those are stolen from the jar while Mom is not looking.

Idea 39: Hourly messages

Details

My partner first did this for me when we were dating. That doesn't mean I cannot revise and turn it into a notable idea of my own, does it?

Locate eight to ten letter-sized envelopes and the same number of sheets of paper. The idea is to give your partner a brief message each hour of the day. Write a note on each piece of paper—I know writing eight to ten notes will be a struggle, but tax yourself a little—and then fold and seal each note within an envelope. Label each envelope with a different hour. Then tell her to open the 12:00 p.m. envelope at precisely 12:00 p.m. and the 1:00 p.m. envelope at 1:00 p.m., and so on. Following so far? That is about it. Straightforward and efficient, isn't it?

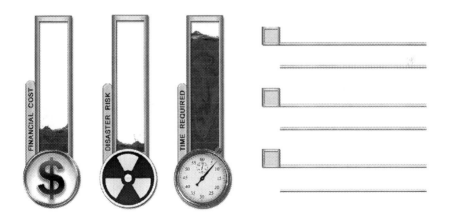

Pitfalls

It might be challenging to think of eight to ten items to compose for this exercise. Look back at the messages illustrated in Idea 10 if you are stuck. Or go to the card shop and copy sappy verses, taking care to dodge the disapproving staff.

Leave a Post-it note on the stack of envelopes that explains what this idea is. Otherwise, you may discover that your surprises have been stamped and tossed into the mailbox.

Extras

Other items can go into the envelopes. If you can line up something special for the evening, it can build up delightful anticipation. I took my partner out to dinner and a musical. There were clues, to that effect, in each of the envelopes she opened throughout the day, and the last one contained the tickets. Be enterprising. Your special treat doesn't have to be a Broadway show, merely something entertaining that she will relish.

Fun Fact 39

The 1912 Olympics was the last one that handed out gold medals that were actually made of gold.

Idea 40: A favorite author

Details

We are already at Idea 40; where does the time go? Do you feel like a romantic wizard yet? You should feel good; hopefully, your faking is going well and benefiting your partner and your marriage.

This idea is actually simple. If your partner likes to read, then she likely has a favorite author or genre. Find out what book she does not have yet, and leave it for her as a surprise.

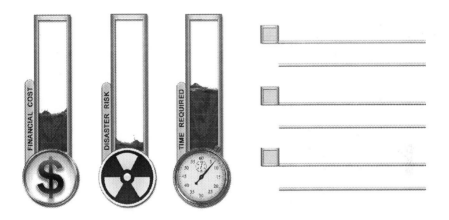

Pitfalls

If she already owns all the books by her favorite author, buy her something from her second-favorite author. Or get a gift certificate that she can use when a new book is released.

If your partner does not take pleasure in books, switch over to plan C and buy one of her favorite magazines or a graphic novel instead.

Extras

Place a romantic bookmark in the publication that you've picked. Most places that sell books or magazines will have little things like that on hand. Consider wrapping the book in nice paper or in a gift bag. Wrapped presents are not just for birthdays but un-birthdays as well. (Confused at that reference? Read *Alice in Wonderland*.)

Of course, once she has her a new tome of literary greatness, she'll need the opportunity to read it. Do the kids need some tending? Could the dishes use a wash? You know what to do.

Fun Fact 40

In Minnesota, citizens may not enter Wisconsin with a chicken on their head. Apparently, they are allowed to cross the road on their way out though.

Idea 41: A sweet on the pillow

Details

Fancy hotels often place a chocolate on their guests' pillows. The better the hotel, the smoother the chocolate (or so the theory goes). If you invest over five hundred dollars a night, you likely will obtain some truly noteworthy chocolate. Anything less than that, and you are better off staying at home and buying a bar for under two dollars.

Buy a classy chocolate, and place it on your partner's pillow so she will spot it when she turns in for the night. Look for a sweet delicacy wrapped in fancy paper that would fit in with a five-hundred-dollars-a-night room. Many fine establishments have temptations that will fit the bill. It is a small way of saying that every day with your partner is a holiday.

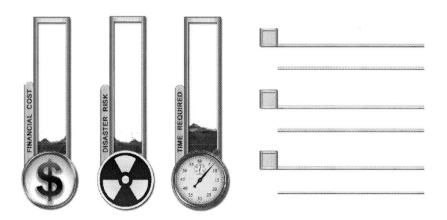

Pitfalls

Again, beware of the diet. If she will not appreciate the chocolate, substitute her favorite candy instead. Of course, it will not have entirely the same effect.

You want to surprise her, so do not put the chocolate on her pillow until you know she is retiring for the night. Do not leave the chocolate out in the sun. Do not let the dog eat it. Use your common sense; it is just a simple chocolate on the pillow! I cannot hold your hand all the time.

Extras

Don't forget to leave that note telling your partner she makes every day a holiday. (Yes, yes, you both know it's not, but it sure sounds charming.)

Have you ever experienced one of those nights together in a hotel? (If you haven't, you should.) Try to create the same effect in your relationship. Occasionally, ship out (or evict) the children, and enjoy a relaxing evening and morning at home instead. If it is a weekend, cook her some breakfast, and make a little holiday out of it. The break will do everyone good (except you, of course, since you are doing all the work, but that's what sacrificial love is all about).

Fun Fact 41

For people who are lactose intolerant, chocolate aids in helping milk digest easier. One more reason to eat more of it.

Idea 42: Movie night

Details

If you have never done this with your partner, then you are missing out on one of life's great simple pleasures. There is nothing quite like snuggling down with your sweetheart, dimming the lights, and losing yourself in her presence and in a great movie.

For this to work well, the children have to be either a) in bed, b) old enough to be kicked out of the house, or c) already married and doing the movie thing themselves. Ensure that there are no other distractions, and then dim the lights and savor the time together.

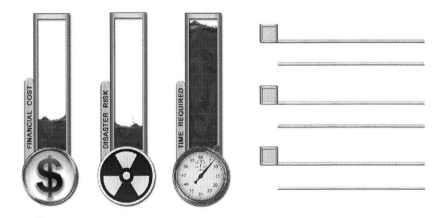

Pitfalls

There are many ways in which this can go wrong, but the most significant one is in the choice of the movie itself. As men, we tend to have our own ideas about what will make the perfect night. However, an evening watching old war movies may not be your partner's idea of a perfect evening. Find something that you both enjoy watching.

My second strong warning: Do not fall asleep during the film. The togetherness part will be lost if you are in dreamland. Finally, do not give a running commentary that makes it clear how fake, silly, pointless, or otherwise uninteresting you find the movie.

Extras

Order in dinner. My partner and I love to spend an evening eating Chinese food and losing ourselves in a good story. Anything you both love will work great. Don't make her work or prepare the food for you. Either do takeout or cook it yourself.

For serious bonus points, ask her to pick the movie she most wants to see. Then sit through it without whining or sleeping. She will love you for showing your "sensitive side."

Fun Fact 42

Director George Lucas has trouble originally getting funding for *Star Wars* because most studios thought audiences wouldn't bother going to see it.

Idea 43: A card with a poem

Details

Cards are wonderful, mostly because of the thought behind the giving and the poem or message inside. Romantic stuff will appeal to your partner because it will make her believe that you have a tender side. By now, you should have convinced her, or almost convinced, her of that.

Instead of a card, look for one of those small cardboard (and sometimes magnetic) items by the checkout stand. They tend to be slightly larger than a business card and have a photo as a background and text in verse or quote format. Find one with a poem or romantic message. Put it on her pillow or plate in the morning.

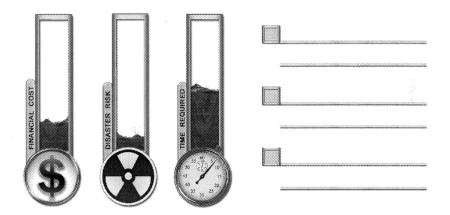

Pitfalls

You shouldn't have too much trouble finding this item; most bookstores and certainly all card shops carry them. Seek and you will find.

Find an appropriate message with a nice picture on it, and you cannot go wrong. Read the entire text as it may contain something you do not mean to say. Some messages can come back to bite you if you are not careful.

Extras

If it had a magnet on the back, she could stick it on the fridge, and that would be rather neat. Isn't science wonderful?

Other than that, take stock of your words of affirmation and praise for your partner. Are you thanking her for the little things she does? Are you reminding her daily that you love her and that she is important to you? Well, get on with it, then!

Fun Fact 43

Someone on Earth reports seeing a UFO every three minutes. Elvis is seen every fifteen minutes … usually in a supermarket.

Idea 44: An e-mail a note

Details

This week, do something really quick and easy. Send your partner an e-mail telling her that you are thinking about her and that you love her. It does not have to be fancy or long—just genuine. If you get stuck trying to figure out what to say there are many romance websites with great verses you can use.

Type your love and press send!

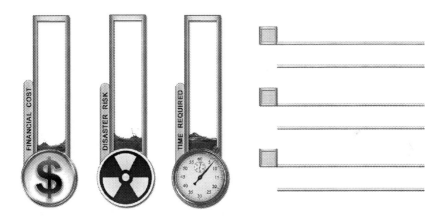

Pitfalls

If your partner does not have an e-mail address, this may be a bit hard. If you have an Internet account but share an e-mail address or do not use e-mail, now would be a great time to encourage your partner to get her own address. Free e-mail accounts are readily available from hotmail.com, yahoo.com, and many other providers.

If you do not have a computer or an Internet connection, grab a pen and paper, and write her a love letter. Leave it where you would have put the computer, if you had one.

Extras

Some wives are less interested in or less informed about the Internet than others. (Of course, some husbands are pretty clueless as well.) It might be nice to teach her or let her teach you about the technology. Why not look into taking a short course together? It might be fun.

> **Fun Fact 44**
>
> The little bags of netting for gas lanterns (called mantles) are radioactive—so much so that they will set off an alarm at a nuclear reactor.

Idea 45: Go out to dinner

Details

We've been through forty-five ideas and you still have not taken her out to dinner? What kind of man are you? Don't you care about her?

Dinners out are great times for couples to reconnect and find a quiet time to talk. I am not talking about dinners with the kids at McDonald's or meals on the run but about a quiet dinner out—just the two of you.

It's your responsibility to find the restaurant, book the sitter (if needed), and surprise her with the idea.

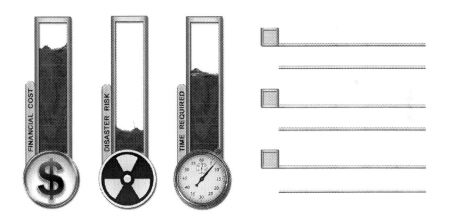

Pitfalls

For many couples, dinner out can add up to a very hefty bill. To cut down on the cost, do not go to a very fancy restaurant. A great burger place can be as intimate and romantic as a restaurant with candles on the tables. Use your imagination and work within your budget.

Do not spring this on your partner as you walk in the door after work. She likely will be a bit upset because she's made dinner already. Give her a day to anticipate and prepare. Planning for a break can be half the fun.

Extras

Giving your partner a card that says "I love you" at dinner will go over well. Conversation about something other than work, kids, sports, or money will be great too. Try to focus your conversation on the two of you. This is a great time to talk about short-term and long-term plans and dreams.

During one dinner, I had the waitress bring my partner a covered dish with her meal. In the dish was a wrapped a pearl necklace. That one paid off for about a month afterward.

Fun Fact 45

In Nebraska, it is illegal for bar owners to sell beer unless they are also brewing a kettle of soup. In some bars, the soup is so bad, it should be illegal to eat it.

Idea 46: A note in a CD case

Details

Most of us listen to music at one time or another during the week. This idea is to hide a note inside something musical for your partner. Write a short note or a simple "I love you" on a piece of paper and slip it into a CD or tape case (if anyone still uses tapes). Leave it for her to find.

Think about putting a date on the note in case it takes a year for your partner to pull out that particular CD.

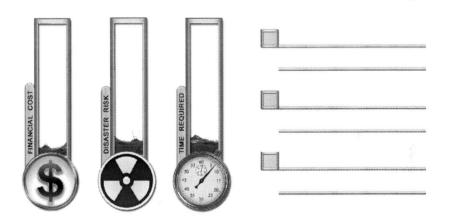

Pitfalls

What if your partner doesn't listen to music? Perhaps the kids do and your partner plays the music for them. Perhaps you could interest her in some music, or ask her to play some of yours one evening.

If your home is totally devoid of music, then try singing loudly and hiding the "I love you" note in your pocket ... or something.

Extras

If she does like music, hiding a note in a *new* CD or tape is a nice way to up the ante. Or put on some appropriate music and have a slow dance with your partner. There are few things as tender and intimate as holding her close and moving slowly to the music.

Fun Fact 46

Sound travels fifteen times faster through steel than through air. However, when a baby cries at night, the sound does not travel far enough to reach the husband's side of the bed.

Idea 47: A small stuffed "something"

Details

When we were kids, most of us had one or more stuffed animals or dolls that were particularly special to us. I do not think we ever grow out of those toys. The sense of security and warmth that once came from that pile of stuffing is incredible. Men generally move past the stuffed animals and start feeling that way about their cars or computers. Many women keep a soft spot for the cute and cuddly.

Find a small stuffed cute thing. Buy it. Put it on your partner's pillow or next to her breakfast plate with a love note.

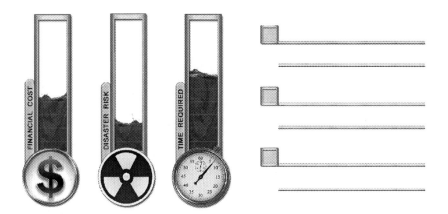

Pitfalls

Some women have no love for stuffed toys. It is a sad state, but it does happen. In that case, perhaps something else will remind her of those warm and fuzzy feelings from her childhood. If she used to cuddle with a socketwrench set, then go and get that for her.

If you have young children, it is important to remind them that the toy "is for Mommy" and not for them. Understand, of course, that they will end up with it regardless. It is the thought that counts, right?

Extras

Stuffed toys were symbols of security for most of us during childhood. Women need to feel secure and safe (often much more so than men). Be aware of your partner's need to feel secure in your love, in your ability to provide for her, and that you respect and admire her. Take the time to remind your partner how special she is to you and how much you cherish her; this week is a good time to whisper those things to her.

Fun Fact 47

In the movie *Babe*, the piglet was played by more than thirty small pigs, since they outgrew the part so quickly during the long production on the film.

Idea 48: A note on her computer screen or behind the screensaver

Details

Most computers contain screensaver software as part of their operating systems. The Windows, Linux, and Mac operating systems all include them. Make sure the screensaver is set, open a new word-processing document or Notepad file, and type a short message of love and affection for your partner. When the note is complete, leave it open on the screen and let the screen saver kick in. The idea is for your partner to find the note on the screen when she sits down to use the computer.

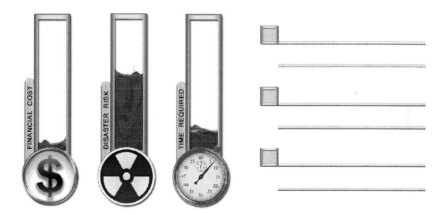

Pitfalls

Do not let one of the kids find the note in which Dad tells Mom that she still has legs that drive him wild. It is not the sort of thing your kids want to experience.

If your partner does not use the computer, then revert to the old Post-it note scheme. Leave it on the microwave or another place she's likely to stumble on it.

Some screensavers include text as part of the display options. Change it to read "Ken loves Joanna." Of course, she might wonder who in the world Ken and Joanna are, if those aren't your names.

Extras

Men often spend a lot of time at the computer screen. Work, play, or school—the computer can use up an incredible amount of our lives. If that is your regular habit, turn off the screen for one night this week, and spend some time with your partner instead. Even if you watch TV (and cuddle), make certain that you do something together.

Fun Fact 48

The first novel ever written on a typewriter was *The Adventures of Tom Sawyer.*

Idea 49: A Post-it note in an oven mitt

Details

This romantic brainwave needs scant explanation. Write a love note and slide it into an oven mitt. The next time she goes to use the mitt, she will feel the paper, pull it out, and find your love and affection waiting for her. It is simple.

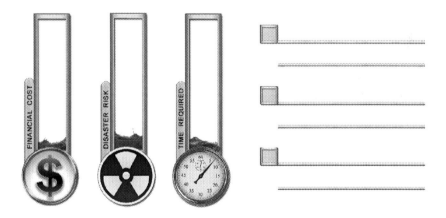

Pitfalls

Do not make the paper so big that she cannot get her hand into the mitt. Do not make it possible for her to lose her grip on the very hot object she is holding. Do not use a pen whose ink quickly melts or runs in the heat.

Extras

Since we are on the topic of heat, how is the passion in your relationship? It can be a challenge to maintain the zest in lovemaking; occasionally, a bit of the unconventional will reignite the spark. The bedroom is not the only room in the house. There are dozens of possible positions. A change of wardrobe can make the familiar seem new. But above all, genuine love, respect, and a man who desires his beloved is the surest aphrodisiac.

Fun Fact 49

Bill Bowerman, co-founder of Nike, got his first shoe idea after staring at a waffle iron. This gave him the idea of using squared spikes to make the shoes lighter.

Idea 50: A snail-mail card, reprised

Details

Sometimes it is not what we receive, but how we receive it that makes the memory. Varying your approaches keeps your legend intact even though you essentially are rehashing the same ideas repeatedly. And women never figure it out. This time, find the strength to go to the card section once again and find a unique card for your partner. This time make it humorous, from one friend to another. A good laugh is beneficial for the soul.

Once you have your card and have written on it, mail it to your partner. For extra fun, do not sign your name or put a return address on it. You might even get someone else to write the note and sign it "A secret admirer."

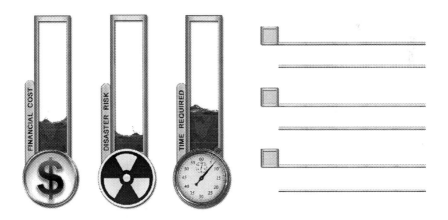

Pitfalls

If you keep forgetting your own address, write it down on something and take it with you. If you cannot stick a stamp on an envelope, ask a friend to assist. Otherwise, it's rather challenging to uncover ways to have this idea cause you grief. You're a pro now; you'll manage.

Extras

Mail one card or note every day of the week, and watch them arrive one by one (or all together two weeks later, depending on the postal service). If one works well, then more should work even better, correct?

If you send out five or more cards, slip a little gift into at least one of them. Even a stick of gum will be appreciated.

Fun Fact 50

"Do not dangle the mouse by its cable, or throw the mouse at co-workers."
from an SGI computer manual

Idea 51: The "key to my heart"

Details

You know the expression, "You have the key to my heart"? Well, if you've never given her the key, now is as good a time as any.

Go to any key-cutting store, and buy a blank and uncut key. Then go to an engraving shop and engrave "Key to my heart" on one side and on the other your name, wedding date, the date you had the key engraved, etc. Or just leave it blank. This little memento will fit nicely on her key ring and bring to mind your love every day.

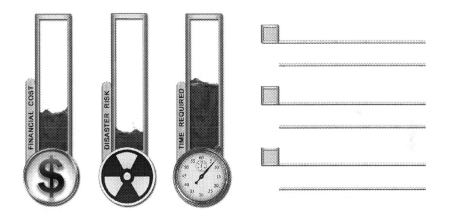

Pitfalls

I can almost guarantee that your partner owns keys. Unless you lock her in the basement (in which case, you are unlikely to be reading this book), she will possess a key ring that can accommodate your token of desire and affection.

Key stores are just about everywhere, and most jewelry stores include inexpensive engraving among their services.

Unless you misplace the key on the way home, this concept is essentially foolproof. It requires a small investment of time, but the financial cost is negligible.

Extras

In some areas of life, presentation is everything. This is undoubtedly true for romance. When I presented my partner with her key many years ago, I also acquired a small jewelry box from the engraver and put the key inside it. Now that I think about it, that was not the greatest idea. She assumed I was buying her jewelry, and when she saw that it was merely a key, she was secretly disappointed. Okay, we have found a new potential pitfall, but if you present it well or place it on her key ring for her to discover, the idea should go over famously. Despite my somewhat awkward presentation, my partner still displays her key (resting in that little box) almost seven years later; not too bad for a few dollars and a little bit of thought.

Fun Fact 51

In 1980, the city of Detroit presented Saddam Hussein with the key to the city. In 1991, the President George H. W. Bush sent in the army, asking for it back. His son finally got the key in 2002. Now you know the real reason for the war.

Idea 52: Flower delivery

Details

If you are doing this in order (and have stayed on schedule), then I assume that there is a slightly wider smile on your face and that you have a happier home life. It is time to celebrate a little, right?

You have relied on flowers in a variety of ways but have not yet had them delivered. Before you shrug off the idea, do not underestimate the power of having someone else unexpectedly bring your partner flowers (as long as you know about it).

Most florists will deliver, and even the floral departments in many grocery stores will as well. Coordinate this well enough in advance to ensure they are delivered when you know she will be at home. Roses are an appropriate flower.

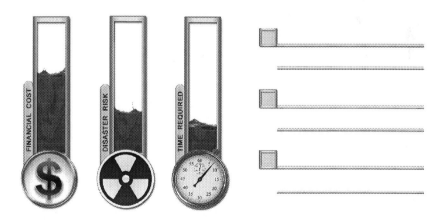

Pitfalls

The expenses are a bit stiffer on this one, but sometimes you have to move away from the "cheap" category and make a serious investment in your continued marital bliss. Resist the impulse to order from a store where you have not purchased flowers before. You want to have some familiarity with the bouquets and services offered. Going into the store in person is a bit easier. However, arranging for the delivery over the phone works as well.

In addition, ensure that she will be home. If the flowers never get into her hands, or the neighbor's dog drags them off and buries them before your partner can find them on the front steps, it will diminish the impact.

In my case, the flowers arrived while my partner was entertaining a few female friends. The positive impression rose exponentially, although I had to hide from the other husbands for a few weeks.

Extras

Pull this off, and you will be "the Man" for a solid week. You are not required to do a lot more, other than congratulate yourself on being so awesome (and remembering all the other little things, but that's getting to be second nature now, correct?).

Fun Fact 52

In 1998, Sony accidently sold 700,000 camcorders that had the technology to see through people's clothes. All have likely been sold on eBay by now.

Idea 53: A recorded message

Details

If you are at all like me, you dislike the sound of your own voice, particularly when it is recorded. This week requires you to overcome that dislike and send a different kind of message to your mate. Instead of writing a note or a poem, make a recording that she can listen to when you are out during the day. It need not be long, but ensure that it is sincere and appropriately tender. Tell her that you want her to hear how much you fancy her.

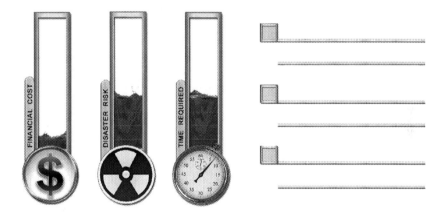

Pitfalls

In the olden days, we accomplished this plan with tape recorders. Making a digital recording and burning it to a CD or saving it to her desktop is far superior in today's day and age; you may no longer even own a tape player or blank cassette. Alternatively, you could leave her a voicemail message of love and devotion. As with other ideas, the risk inherent in having someone other than your intended recipient hear your message will depend on its content. Use your own discretion.

Extras

Perhaps it is time to introduce some new music into the house. Find out what type of music your partner enjoys (if you still do not know) and bring home a CD or download it to her iPod or MP3 player. Music can have an amazing effect. If you are going for broke, buy her a CD player (if she does not already have one), or upgrade the one she has.

Fun Fact 53

Cats can make over a hundred different vocal sounds; dogs can make about ten. Women tend to prefer cats, and men tend to prefer dogs. However, there is no correlation between those two facts.

Idea 54: A heart drawn in the sand, snow, or dirt

Details

This task is possibly the simplest one yet presented. Venture outside. Sketch a heart shape in the sand, dirt, or snow (depending on the weather and place where you reside). Place your initials within the heart, and leave the sketch for her to find.

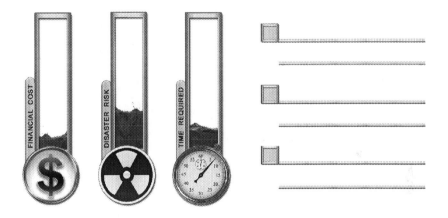

Pitfalls

If there is no dirt, sand, or snow outside, perhaps you could mow a heart into the lawn (your own, not the neighbor's). Or you could draw it on the road with chalk.

Rain, children, pets, or sudden windstorms might erase your masterpiece before she sees it. Try to ensure that she finds her way to the window or goes outside and sees it before it is lost forever.

Extras

Hearts in the dirt may not be a magnum opus but they certainly can create good memories. Why not take some time to sit down with your partner and look at your albums or home movies? Recalling pleasant events can set the tone for the future. Put on some music, brew some coffee or tea, and invest a little time in reminiscing.

Fun Fact 54

The revenue that is generated from gambling is more than that from movies, cruise ships, recorded music, theme parks, and spectator sports combined.

Idea 55: A large balloon

Details

You have used balloons before, but this time you are aiming bigger and grander. Get the largest balloon you can find. It can have a pre-printed message on it, or you can write your own. Hide it in the car, the minivan, or the house for your partner to discover. Perhaps your message could say: "My love for you just keeps growing and growing."

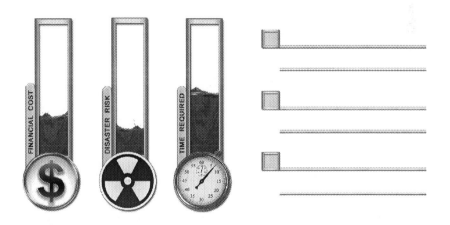

Pitfalls

Make sure you can get the balloon into the vehicle. Try not to pop it (or let the cat at it). You should be able to manage the rest. Oh, and do not write, "My love and your hips just keep growing and growing."

Extras

Balloons bring to mind hot air. It is very easy to wound with our words. Muttered comments and hurtful stories about our partners to friends can tear down instead of build up our mates. The tongue is a deadly thing when used to hurt. This week, make a point of building your partner up with your words. Encourage her. Make a strong commitment to refrain from criticizing or ridiculing her, particularly in front of others. If your partner tears you down, let her know how much it hurts you. If you are following the ideas in this book in order, I expect that your partner's attitude toward you has softened a whole lot.

Fun Fact 55

Race-car driver Lee Petty once left a pit stop and did a full lap with a member of the pit crew on the hood. I don't think that a simple "Sorry" was sufficient.

Idea 56: A gift certificate for a back rub

Details

The back-rub notion is not unique. However, instead of merely offering to give your partner a back rub after a hard day, present her with a gift certificate for one instead. Whether you purchase, construct, print, or copy the certificate, make sure she can redeem it whenever the need arises. The more creative you are the better, but if you are looking for ideas, the Internet is sure to have some you can print out and use.

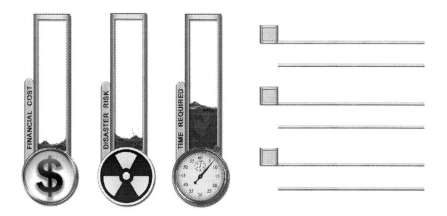

Pitfalls

Offers for back rubs usually are not met with resistance. There should be no complications associated with this idea. If your partner, for some reason, does not want/need a back rub now and again, then substitute a foot or leg massage, or a massage of some other part of her body. I will leave the decision up to you.

It might be a good idea to do this when the kids are in bed or when the company has left, but I am sure you figured that part out already.

Extras

If she is receptive to the idea, then begin at the back and work your way from there. A full-body massage can be simply sublime. Ensure that you have the time to do it well and without complaint. If your hands start to ache or you get tired, suck it up and press on. Since you are a manly man, you should have no difficulties. When our kids were very young, and unlikely to get out of bed and come down the stairs, I set up an impromptu massage parlor in our living room. A few foam mattresses, an old, clean comforter, some towels, candles, music, and massage oil were all that I needed. It was a good evening.

Fun Fact 56

Rats multiply so quickly that in eighteen months, two rats could have over a million descendants. The Dutch take only slightly longer.

Idea 57: A movie purchase

Details

Not everyone loves movies, but I suspect that most people appreciate at least one film or film genre. Many women like romantic comedies or dramas. Each to their own, I suppose.

This week, buy your partner a movie on DVD, Blu-ray, or digital download. Make certain it is one she truly fancies and will wish to view again. You could also watch it with her.

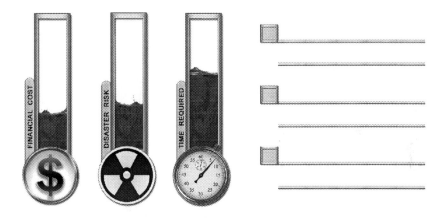

Pitfalls

Some individuals genuinely hate movies of all kinds. I've not encountered any of these people, but I read about them in a book once. If this is true of your partner, buy her a printed work instead. Similarly, if you do not have a DVD or a Blu-ray player, you may need to resort to a book. You also could take your partner to see a movie or a play. Find something that works within one of those parameters, and you are sure to score some points.

Do not bring home *The Hurt Locker* or *Saving Private Ryan,* unless you are completely positive that your partner loves war movies, and I mean totally and utterly positive.

Extras

Make popcorn, order in something, or determine some other way to pamper your partner while the movie is playing. Perhaps you could help with something around the house (the dishes, putting the kids to bed, etc.), so that she has the time and energy to unwind and enjoy the film.

Fun Fact 57

The name for Oz, in *The Wizard of Oz,* was thought up when creator Frank Baum looked at his filing cabinet. He saw A–N and O–Z. Oz it was.

Idea 58: An indoor picnic

Details

The originality of this idea stems from its venue. Instead of a picnic outside, have one inside. Spread out a blanket on the floor, pack a picnic basket; then invite your partner to sit with you on the floor and munch something palatable. This works especially well in the winter, when a picnic out-of-doors is simply not sensible. It is a noteworthy way to bring a momentary bit of sunshine to an otherwise cold and dreary day. If your partner suffers from the "winter blues," this can be particularly effective.

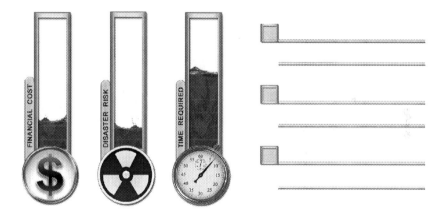

Pitfalls

Be sure to use a blanket on the floor to protect it (or the carpet) from stains and spills. (If they do occur, then who do you think should volunteer to clean?) Ensure that the contents of the picnic are provisions your partner enjoys. If you do not have a picnic basket, then use a box or simply set everything on the blanket in advance.

Extras

For extra mood and effect, have the picnic after dark and light some candles or the fire. Soft music will enhance the mood. Some couples will take turns feeding each other, although that may have an unpleasant outcome. For example, I heard about an incident involving excessively low lighting and misplaced potato salad.

Fun Fact 58

Franklin D. Roosevelt's three favorite foods were frog legs, pig knuckles, and scrambled eggs—none of which are good foods for picnics.

Idea 59: "I love you"
in different languages

Details

On a piece of paper, or a series of Post-it notes, write down the following phrases:

I love you	– English
Je t'aime	– French
Ya loblow tebya	– Russian
Aku cinta padamu	– Indonesian
Ti amo	– Italian
Te quiero	– Spanish
Ik heb je lievte	– Dutch
Jag alskar dig	– Swedish
Jacie kocham	– Polish
Seni seviyorum	– Turkish
Ngoh oi nei	– Cantonese
Eu te amo	– Portuguese

Then add: "No matter how I express it, it all means the same thing: I love you!" Once that is accomplished, take the piece of paper (or the Post-it notes), and place where your partner will find it. She will marvel at your effort and research, and the message will be much appreciated.

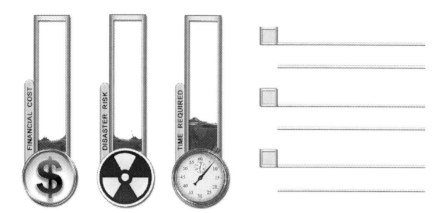

Pitfalls

Since I have already provided the list of phrases, all you have to do is write it out and place it somewhere. It is not an arduous task and one that you can accomplish without undue strain. As always, keep the paper out of the reach of pets and children; they are small but also destructive.

Extras

This week, learn a foreign language and compose a song for your bride in a new tongue. Does that sound too overwhelming? Okay, let us think about something that is a little simpler. Tell your partner that you love and cherish her. Do an internal evaluation to see if your gestures and words are genuine. Faking romance is one thing, but faking love is something else all together, and I don't endorse the latter.

Fun Fact 59

During his or her lifetime, the average human will grow 590 miles of hair. Most men comb 400 miles of it; women style well over 2,000 miles' worth.

Idea 60: A facial or pedicure

Details

Everyone appreciates being pampered, men included (particularly if it means being served a cold beer and a bag of chips by Swedish models in bikinis). Since women ordinarily give more thought and consideration to their physical appearance and body, give your partner the opportunity for a little pampering. Remember the massage you gave her? Keep that vibe rolling. This time, get her a gift certificate for a professional massage, facial, manicure, pedicure, or whatever else you think she will like best. Most towns with more than one hundred people have some variety of spa that offers such services.

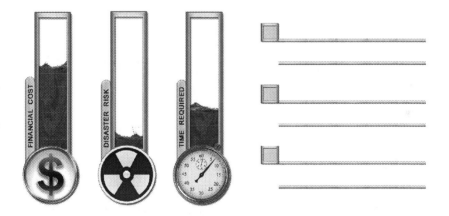

Pitfalls

Get her something she likes. If she abhors having her feet touched, do not get a certificate for a pedicure. Make certain she does not have to drive for hours to get there, or she will need a full-body massage as well as the pedicure. Ensure that she can pick a time to use the services at her discretion, so she does not have to discard all her other plans.

Extras

Perhaps she would like to go to the spa with a friend. Spa treatments usually are both rejuvenating and socially stimulating experiences. If her friend is married, suggest to her husband that he follow your example. If he's not persuaded this is a good idea, let him borrow this book (but only for a moment because he should purchase his own copy). Make sure that someone is watching the kids, if necessary, as well.

Fun Fact 60

Betsy Ross was born with a fully formed set of teeth. Her other contribution to the American Revolution, besides sewing the first American flag, was running a munitions factory in her basement.

Idea 61: "Lucky in love"
written on a clover leaf

Details

The four-leaf clover is a symbol of good luck. Whether or not you believe in the concept of luck, this idea likely will bring a smile to her face. (We will leave the discussion of the abstract topic of luck to another book. We are interested only in practical details and results).

Since it is difficult to find a genuine four-leaf clover, construct one out of green paper. Once you have cut out your clover, write, "Darling, I'm lucky in love because I have you." Plant it somewhere for her to unearth, and you are all set.

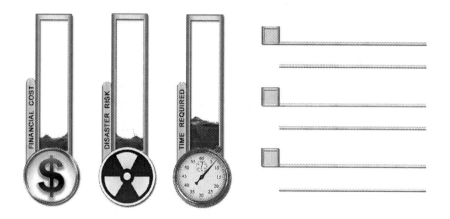

Pitfalls

It may be tough to sketch a good four-leaf clover. I personally have very pitiable artistic skills. Fortunately, Google exists, and you can find a template to copy online. In a worst-case scenario (nuclear war, no computers), just wing it; if it is close enough, she'll get the message. You also want to be careful when using the scissors. Do not use a band saw to cut the paper. Bigger is not always better.

Extras

Contemplating luck often reminds me of board games and card games. Do you and your bride ever play such games, either together or with the kids? Games can be a first-rate way to spend time together and enjoy each other's company since you can be involved in an activity and converse at the same time. If your partner agrees to late-night strip poker, so much the better.

Fun Fact 61

Los Angeles's full name is "El Pueblo Nuestra Senora la Reina de los Angeles de Porciuncula." It can be abbreviated to 3.63 percent of its original size: "L.A."

Idea 62: A virtual florist

Details

You have sent flowers, brought flowers, left flowers, and delivered flowers already. One thing you have not done is send an e-flower. Just like an e-card, an e-flower is a quick and simple gesture of love and affection for your partner. Just point your Web browser to www.virtualflorist. com, and send your partner an e-flower bouquet. It is quick, simple, and free.

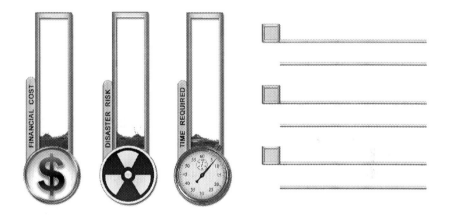

Pitfalls

Those without a computer, e-mail, or Internet access are going to find this idea a little harder to accomplish than the rest of us. Rather than going out and buying a computer, why not substitute a real flower for the electronic one? Leave it for her to find, or surprise her with it when you come home from work.

Extras

A nice note with the e-flower would be nice, something meaningful and genuine, of course.

Fun Fact 62

At 120 miles per hour, a Formula One car generates so much downforce that it can drive upside down on the roof of a tunnel.

Idea 63: A puzzle created
with a photo or message

Details

Since love is often a puzzle (and people invariably are), how better to demonstrate your love than with a literal one? There are a variety of ways to employ this idea, depending on your creativity and energy. The easiest option is to write a message of love on a section of cardboard, and then cut it into distinctive shapes. Leave the shapes in a pile, and ask your partner put the puzzle together. To take this idea one step further, print out an image or message on card stock at a local copy shop and do the cutting task yourself. Or have a photo-development place produce the puzzle for you. This last suggestion provides the most impact but also the greatest expense.

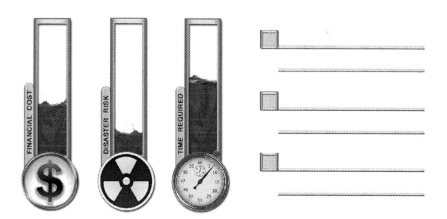

Pitfalls

Do not make a puzzle that consists of three hundred tiny pieces. She probably won't make the effort to put it together just to see a little message. Ten to twenty-five pieces should do well for a homemade puzzle. A few more are okay if it is professionally made. Do not lose any pieces before she gets a chance to make it. Do not cut yourself with the scissors. Do not let the dog eat the paper. You get the idea.

Extras

This week, try to approach life and love with the attitude that it is all a game. Often, we get far too serious about relationships; while they need work, they should not feel like work. Do something fun with your partner. Anything will do, as long as it involves time together and lots of happy smiles. (How happy the smile is up to you. Nudge, nudge, wink, wink.)

Fun Fact 63

The parents of Albert Einstein were worried that he was mentally slow because it took him a long time to learn to speak.

Idea 64: A Scrabble message

Details

This idea might take a bit of pre-planning, but since you likely are reading ahead, you have sufficient time to prepare. The idea itself is simple: locate an old Scrabble game at a garage sale, second-hand shop, or thrift store. In a pinch, use the family Scrabble game if you already have one at home. Take out the letters and form the words "I love you" in a classic Scrabble pattern. (For example, the word "you" can intersect with the word "love" and share the "o.") If you want, get a bit more complex and construct a longer message. Leave the Scrabble message where she will find it. If you buy an old version of the game, consider gluing the pieces to a nice bit of finished wood, which will transform this simple idea into a real keepsake.

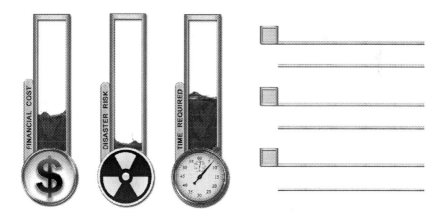

Pitfalls

Not knowing how to spell could be a pitfall. I have written the message out for you though, so merely follow the letters. Don't leave the Scrabble note where the kids, dog, or in-laws will find and/or remove it. Make sure small children or pets do not chew or choke on the letters. Do not glue the pieces onto the game board as that will make playing the game more difficult.

Extras

Last time, you did something fun with your partner. Hopefully, that worked out famously and a fabulous time was had by all. This time, to avoid causing strain, we'll leave the task as is. If, however, you feel motivated to show a little extra love, support, friendship, and tenderness to your partner, then do not let me stop you.

Fun Fact 64

Farmers in England are required by law to provide their pigs with toys. However, the pigs are not allowed to possess copies of *Animal Farm*.

Idea 65: A cook-out on a camp stove at the beach

Details

This idea requires some preparation. It cannot be done in a commercial break, but a few commercial breaks should be enough time. Since it needs to be done outside, it also is best attempted during the spring, summer, or early fall (depending on where you live).

Pick up some food at the grocery store, the kind of things that you can prepare on a camp stove. You are going to have a picnic on the beach, and you are going to cook for her, for a change (perhaps). You can boil vegetables, fry some chicken, heat up an instant camping dinner—whatever you think she will fancy and that you can manage. Cook for her, enjoy the time out together, and do the cleanup yourself. If you locate a suitably romantic spot, the ambiance will do most of the work.

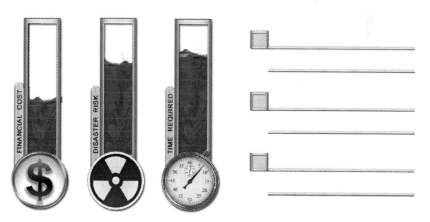

Pitfalls

There are quite a few possible pitfalls associated with this idea, so be aware. If you do not have a camp stove, borrow or buy one. Stoves tend to get hot, so do not burn yourself or set any nearby grass on fire. Do not spill the food into the dirt. Cook something she will actually eat. If you cook something like hamburger or pork, make sure it is cooked properly. Nothing ruins a good romantic idea like a little food poisoning.

Extras

If you pull this one off well, you will be "the Man" again for at least a few weeks. What else do you need to do? Pat yourself on the back, and take the rest of the week off. However, I encourage you to consider your food choices carefully. There is significant room for creativity and lasting memories here.

Fun Fact 65

Some ribbon worms will eat themselves if they can't find any food. That pretty much guarantees a permanent solution to the problem.

Idea 66: A bookmark in a favorite book

Details

This week, you probably are searching for a manageable plan. This one is spartan, but do not underestimate its potential. All small gestures are appreciated by nearly all women.

Find or make a bookmark, and slip it into a book or magazine your partner is currently reading. Buy one from a card or bookstore, or cut out and decorate a piece of cardboard and make your own. Put messages of love and affirmation on it, and slip it in the book.

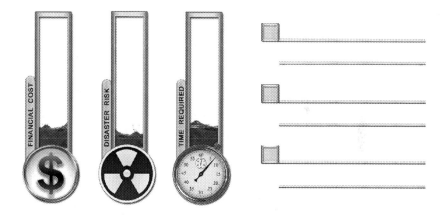

Pitfalls

There's no danger of anything catching fire this time, so you are safe in that way. Other than a paper cut, there is little risk or much that can go awry. Simply make sure the bookmark is nice and that she can find it.

Extras

It is time for some extra credit. Does your partner have enough free time for reading? Could she use a little break or some quiet time? This is your cue to make sure she gets it. Whether that means doing the dishes or putting the kids to bed, show her how much you appreciate what she does. I realize that this is familiar ground, and perhaps you're weary of it by now. However, marriage isn't a sprint, it's a marathon, so press onward. You only stop loving when you stop breathing, right?

Fun Fact 66

It is not possible to tickle yourself. The cerebellum warns the rest of the brain that you are about to. Since your brain knows this, it ignores the sensation.

Idea 67: A customized comic strip

Details

It is my goal to provide numerous formats in which you can express your delight in your mate, and this one ranks high on the originality scale. You may not have attempted something of this nature before but, thanks to modern technology, it is not difficult. Point your Web browser at www.stripcreator.com, and click on the "make a comic" link. This marvelous, free little site allows you to create a three-panel comic strip, utilizing a variety of characters, backgrounds, and effects. The particular content of your comic remains your choice, though two characters (one of whom is you, perhaps) talking about how wonderful their partners are might be a good place to begin.

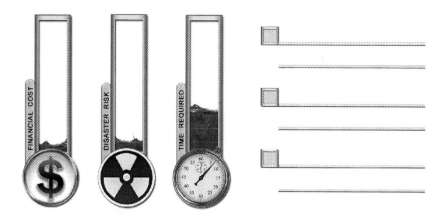

Pitfalls

Granted, generating the content of the comic strip likely will be the largest obstacle, so some time may be required for a good idea to form. The actual presentation of the comic strip itself should prove no great challenge. Simply print the page when done, crop as required, and present to her via the method of your choice.

Since I do not own or run this particular site, I cannot guarantee that it will exist forever. Nevertheless, a quick Google search undoubtedly will provide some alternatives should this one vanish.

Extras

If you are feeling particularly ambitious, create a short series of strips. You also could find out which comic was her childhood favorite and purchase an anthology of those strips. Most popular strips have been published in book format.

Fun Fact 67

The Danish company, Lego, which began in 1932, first manufactured ironing boards and stepladders. It is unlikely that they have ever looked back.

Idea 68: A day taking the kids out

Details

If you have children, and your spouse spends a significant amount of her time at home with them, it might earn you bonus points to take them off her hands for a day. It can be either a Saturday or a weekday, but the objective is to give your partner a day off and enable her to spend some time doing things she enjoys, or needs to get done, minus any "little distractions."

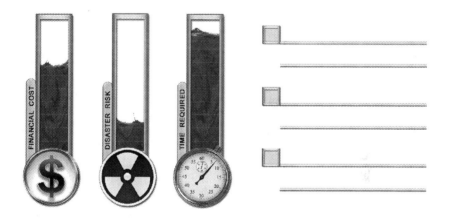

Pitfalls

If you do not have offspring, or the kids already have houses of their own, this idea will be more challenging to accomplish. You could possibly take the dog or cat out for the day. If that will not work either, then roll up your sleeves and take care of some of the duties that need to get accomplished. You also could suggest that she take a girlfriend out to lunch. Then they can spend the time talking about how awesome you are.

Extras

I hope I do not have to remind you of the need to pitch in when it is needed. I thought not. Carry on, then.

Fun Fact 68

During the Renaissance, people believed that walnuts could cure head ailments since their shape was similar to a brain. They were nuts.

Idea 69: A surprise lunch

Details

Most women love to be surprised, as long as the surprise is a pleasant one. "Hey, honey, I bought a sports car" is unlikely to be placed within that category. This idea involves surprising her at home or work and taking her out to lunch. It does not have to be a grand and complex affair, but a slice of time together in the middle of the day is a nice novelty for many couples.

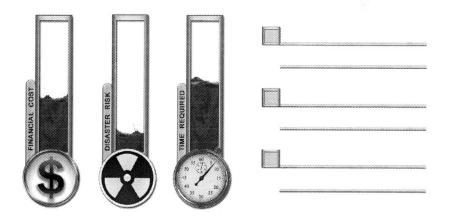

Pitfalls

Children may be a factor here, and you either will have to take them with you (bleh), or find someone to watch them. Furthermore, if you work a considerable distance from your partner and it will take some time to get to her, then this plan will not succeed easily. You could theoretically take a "sick day," but I do not wish to encourage that (or so my lawyer cautions me). As a last-ditch concept, you could have lunch delivered to your partner at home or the office, or give her a gift certificate to a favorite restaurant. Then she can go there herself, although the ideal is for you to do this together.

Extras

Surprising her in person doubtlessly will have the greatest impact. Expend the extra effort required to make that happen, and you are all set. Of course, make sure you select food that she likes; my future bride told me she hated Mexican food but only after the meal was over. Consider going to a venue that is at least one step up from fast food. Happy Meals are renowned but not particularly romantic to anyone over the age of five.

Fun Fact 69

Alfred Hitchcock did not have a belly button for much of his life. It was eliminated when he was sewn up after a surgery.

Idea 70: A poem in parts, on different hidden cards

Details

Find or compose a poem for your mate. If the word poetry causes you distress, there are many great collections of love poems in bookstores, local libraries, or on the Internet. You should be able to find at least one good one without too much trouble. Write each line (or section, if it is a long poem) on a separate piece of paper. Number each paper so that when she finds them she will be able to put them in order. Then hide the papers throughout the house in places where she will stumble upon them throughout the day. Hopefully, by the evening she will have assembled and been suitably impressed by your poem and effort.

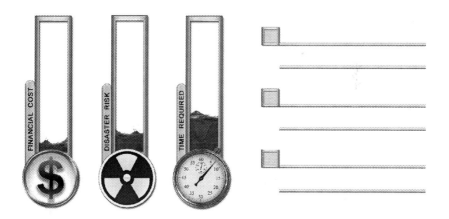

Pitfalls

The sickly-sweet and formulaic poetry of Helen Steiner Rice should be avoided. Not being able to locate a notable poem might be considered a pitfall. However, with so many avenues and ways to uncover at least one suitable candidate, that is hardly a valid excuse. As with the other ideas that involve penmanship, you will have to ensure it is legible or typed. Other than that little speed bump, I am sure you will manage.

Extras

Write the poem yourself. Enough said.

Fun Fact 70

In Massachusetts, it is illegal to frighten a pigeon. However, if you can shoot it without scaring it, all is well. Except for the pigeon, of course, which is dead.

Idea 71: Cutout hearts
hung from the ceiling

Details

Remember that scene in the movie *Seven* when Brad Pitt and Morgan Freeman walk into a room where all the air fresheners are hanging from the ceiling? If you do, try to forget it; it's rather disturbing. However, that scene does form the basis for this idea.

To effect this plan, cut out a heart (or rather a number of hearts) from red paper and write "I love you" on each one. Then take a hole puncher and punch out a hole at the top. Use a bit of string and either tacks or tape to suspend the hearts from the ceiling. This is a unique and surprising way to tell her of your love; the more hearts, the merrier.

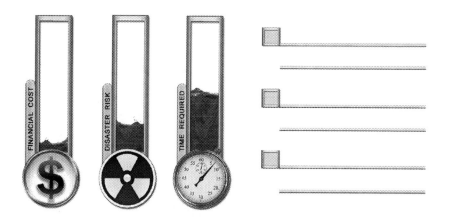

Pitfalls

Similar to the clover idea, cutting and basic artistic skills are required. For people like me, that's a significant challenge, but one can overcome that by tracing or printing a heart shape off the computer. It worked for the clover leaves, and it will work for hearts as well. There's no need to start saving pictures of diamonds and spades; we're not going to use them for anything.

Do not put tacks or tape anywhere where they won't come out or off easily, or where they will do permanent damage. If the house is not suitable, then make the strings smaller and hang them inside the car.

Extras

To see these notices of love, she will have to look up. "Looking up" is a term used to refer to someone's mood or spirits. This week your auxiliary task is to lift your partner's spirits in some fashion. Make her laugh, give her specific words of encouragement, determine some way to boost her up.

Whatever you do, watch your choice of words, especially around other people. Do you fire little barbs at your partner, whether the two of you are alone or with others? Isn't it time to make a solid commitment to stop?

Fun Fact 71

One of the steepest main streets in Canada is located in Saint John, New Brunswick. Over a distance of two blocks the street rises about eighty feet.

Idea 72: Flowers with notes on the stems

Details

Giving her flowers is not original, but this is a variation on the theme. This idea functions best with flowers that do not include thorns, so do not choose roses for this occasion. Write messages of love or affirmation on small strips of paper. If you can come up with something original, so much the better; if not, the card aisle is calling you.

Wrap the messages around the stem of each flower. If you obtain a dozen flowers, you will need a dozen messages. Use a small piece of tape to stick them to the stems. You want her to be able to take off the messages without a knife. You also can tape the messages in such a way that they look like little flags. In that case, she will be able to read your messages without unrolling them. The key here is to not make this an onerous task for her.

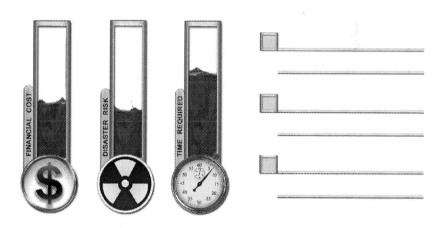

Pitfalls

Do not let the messages become wet by dropping the flowers into water before she gets a chance to read your notes. Make sure the notes do not fall off the second you move the flowers more than a few inches. When it comes to flowers, you should be a pro by now.

Extras

Seven days in a week ... one flower and message left for her each day ... Hmm.

Fun Fact 72

In February of 1878, the first telephone book was published in New Haven, Connecticut. The book was one page long and had fifty names in it. Women wanted to talk to every person in the book.

Idea 73: "I love you" business cards

Details

Everyone has a business card these days. Even people who do not work seem to have a card. Your partner is going to get a business card too; in fact, she is going to get a whole collection of cards. Come up with something you fancy to say on a card—how about "I love you! ... and I can't say it enough"?—and get one hundred or more of them printed. Then, conceal them around the house so she will find them gradually. This time, hide at least some of them in obscure spots. That way, there is a good chance that your partner still will be discovering the odd one even a month later. This is a plan that can last weeks, if it is done well.

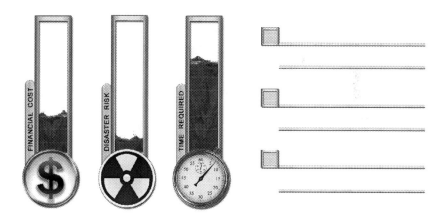

Pitfalls

This might appear formidable, but it is not all that challenging. Black-and-white business cards are very inexpensive to print, and there are numerous locations that will create them. Make up the phrase, have the cards printed, and hide them around the house. How hard can that be?

Extras

If she is still finding the cards more than a month later, you will earn bonus points. Of course, you could regularly tell your partner that you love her (and mean it).

Fun Fact 73

Astronaut Buzz Aldrin's mother's name was Moon. Buzz was the second man to step onto the moon in 1976.

Idea 74: A note of affirmation

Details

Compose a note that says the following:

Your conversation interests me.

Your laughter delights me.

Your love completes me.

Your hugs warm me.

Your kisses enflame me.

Your talks encourage me.

Your touch soothes me.

Your dedication inspires me.

Your support propels me.

Your prayers quiet me.

Your friendship means the world to me.

Write the words above on a piece of paper; leave it for her.

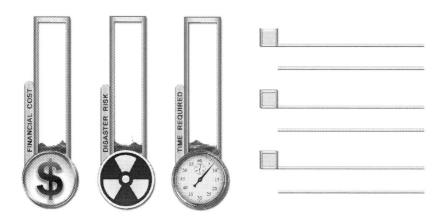

Pitfalls

Unless you cannot write or do not have paper, you will sort this one out quite quickly.

Extras

Print on nice parchment paper. Add a few messages of your own to the list. Put it on a plaque, in wood, or carved into glass; use your imagination. Many engraving shops include a wide selection of materials that can enhance your words. Depending on how permanent you want this to be, there are numerous opportunities.

Fun Fact 74

A young heir to a sausage empire was fined £116,000 for driving at 50 mph in a 25 mph zone. Speeding tickets in Finland are based on annual income levels, and not on a flat rate. If you are unemployed and you speed, the government pays you.

Idea 75: Messages throughout the day

Details

This idea works best on a Saturday or a holiday, though any day on which neither of you have to go to work should suffice. Create three sets of envelopes with ideas of things to do and/or places to eat. Give them to your partner at the beginning of the day. During the day, she will select one envelope from each set, and you will do what it says.

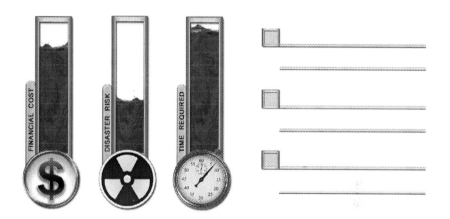

Pitfalls

Think this one through and do not list any options that you or she will not want to do. Take into account travel time and costs; there likely will be a few other factors as well. However, do not let that daunt you. Expend a little bit of time on this one, and you will have a wonderful day filled with excitement and surprise for both of you.

Extras

Doing this one well will require a bit of planning and effort. That's enough of a strain, don't you think?

Fun Fact 75

A female ferret will often die if she goes into heat and cannot find a mate. Males (among ferrets and most other species) only think they will.

Idea 76: Comments in a magazine

Details

This idea is unpretentious but effective. Grab a few Post-it notes, and find a magazine that your partner is reading or will read within the next few days. If the magazine has any pictures of attractive women (and most do ... look at the ads), then put a Post-it note on that page. Write something like, "Poor gal ... it's a shame, she's not half as lovely as you." Or "Some will think she's pretty, but I know <u>you're</u> gorgeous." If you are not feeling quite that valiant, "I love you" will work in a pinch. The general idea is to compare another woman to your partner and tell her that, in your eyes, she is higher up on the scale.

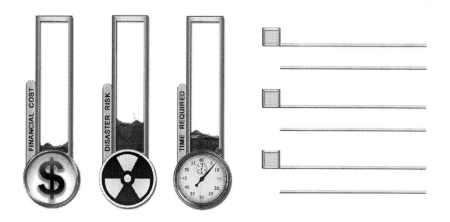

Pitfalls

This idea requires an understanding of your partner's emotional barometer, her perceptions of the way she looks, and her perceptions of other women. A light-hearted note may succeed for some women; for others, something more solemn is needed. Hopefully, you have been studying your partner and are learning what makes her tick. Use your head, and write what will connect with her.

If your partner does not have a magazine, then put the note in a book, bible, TV Guide, or whatever else she's reading. Understand, however, that the message in combination with an image of a model is the intent.

Extras

Purchase a magazine that you know she will like and leave the notes in it beforehand. Perhaps leave it as a surprise for her to find in the morning or at night. That is one certain way to ensure she'll see your comments.

Fun Fact 76

A squash ball moving at 93 mph (150 kph) has the same impact as a .22 caliber bullet. However, it's not likely to leave a hole in you.

Idea 77: An unusual flower pot

Details

If your partner has a sweet tooth, then this idea is sure to be a hit. If she does not, then she likely will keep your creation longer, and it will have an extended impact. Either way, you can't lose. Here is what you need to do:

Go to a flower shop or a store like Home Depot. Buy a small flower pot, preferably made of clay and not plastic, and one or more silk flowers. Clean and fill the pot with chocolate-covered raisins and/ or peanuts, and stick in the silk flower(s). You may have to trim the stems down to make it to look good. Write on the pot: "Your love is the sweetest thing."

The candy is the "dirt"; get it? For greater impact, add some Gummi worms to the pot.

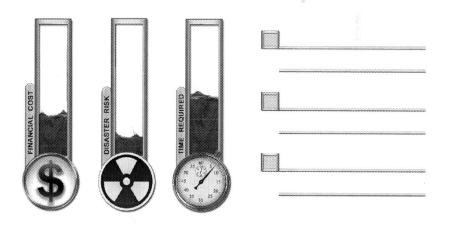

Pitfalls

Keep the flower pot out of the reach of kids and pets. If they get at it first, you will find that the "dirt" level has mysteriously subsided. Finding the right pot and flower(s) and writing the message nicely will take a bit of work. However, you really cannot call a wee bit of effort a pitfall anymore, so do not use that as an excuse. A good felt-tip marker will write nicely on the pot, so that portion of the plan should come off without a hitch.

If your partner hates chocolate-covered raisins, then look for other alternatives. Perhaps chocolate ice cream would work; you'll have to serve that to her at the just right time, however. Other ideas are possible. Use your imagination.

Extras

Painting the words will enhance the pot. Craft stores are ideal places for finding letter templates or a staff person who can do the painting for you. You also can try to find chocolate roses and make them part of your edible display. Anything to enhance the presentation and, thus, its reception, will be splendid.

Fun Fact 77

On average, 42,000 balls are used and 650 matches are played at the annual Wimbledon tennis tournament.

Idea 78: A note in a pocket

Details

Because you have done a significant amount of creative work in the past few weeks, it is time to do something slightly easier. After all, this book is all about simple ideas, right? In that spirit, this exercise is as simple as it gets. When your partner takes a shower or disappears into the bathroom in the morning, slip a simple "I love you" note into the pocket of the clothes she will wear that day. What could be simpler?

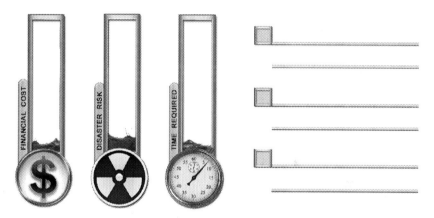

Pitfalls

You may not know what she plans to wear. It is also possible that she has no idea what she will wear either. Perhaps she does not lay out her clothes before she heads to the shower. If that is the case, just wing it. Place the note in a piece of clothing she is likely to wear within the next few days. If she does not discover it immediately, she will undoubtedly do so later.

However, do not slip it into a pocket of something that is about to go into the wash.

Extras

Instead of a simple note, write a short letter or poem. Again, the card aisle and the Internet can provide you with a number of suitable and sappy things for which you can claim credit. Nice paper, instead of a Post-it or scrap of paper, is also an interesting addition.

Fun Fact 78

An apple, potato, and onion all taste the same if you eat them with your nose plugged. They all taste sweet.

Idea 79: A small gift basket

Details

Getting pampered is always pleasant; this time you are going to give your partner something with which to pamper herself. Somewhere near where you reside, there is likely The Body Shop or some other store that sells products that aid the pampering process. Oils, lotions, creams, buffers, cleaners, shiners, exfoliates, and other strange substances will be at your fingertips. Buy a variety of small things, place them in a decorative box or basket, and give it to your partner as a surprise.

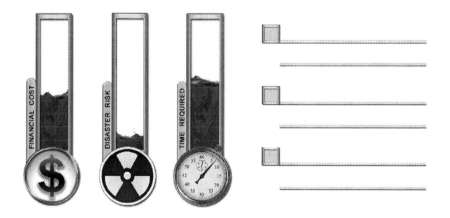

Pitfalls

If you are at all like me, these products are completely foreign to you. That is why most of these stores have helpful sales assistants who will be overjoyed to recommend items that fall within your plans and budget. Often, they will wrap it up nicely for you as well. What could be simpler? (Not doing it at all does not count!)

Extras

You know what I am going to say here, don't you? Then, I do not have to say it.

> **Fun Fact 79**
>
> Atari had to bury over five million unsold or returned "E.T." video game cartridges in a landfill in New Mexico. Yes, the game was that bad.

Idea 80: A scavenger hunt

Details

Most people participated in some type of scavenger hunt when they were kids. This idea is designed to bring that fun back into focus for a short while. You will need several items for this to work. First, you'll need a worthwhile prize for your partner to find at the conclusion of the hunt. Second, you'll need a list of clues, one leading to another, ending up at whatever treasure you acquire.

It is primarily the clues that make this idea both functional and fun. Outright directions—go to the car, look under the mat—are functional enough but rather deficient in the fun category. Clues should require moderate pondering and puzzling to sort out. As a rule, I would recommend no more than five to eight clues. Too many, and she may tire of the exercise. Too few, and it will be over far too fast.

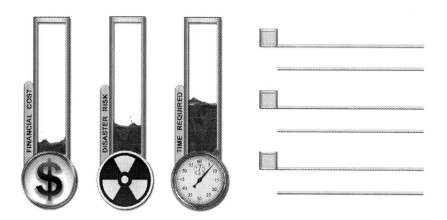

Pitfalls

Do not make the clues so obscure that they will be indecipherable without assistance. If she cannot figure them out, it will not be any fun. Do not put the prize in a location she will not be able to get to. It might seem like a good idea to stage the grand finale on the roof of the barn, but it's not.

If you don't know what to write on the clues, ask a female friend for help. (You don't want your male friends to discover your romantic activities, even faked ones).

Extras

The grander the prize at the end, the better. While I recommend that it be something larger than a chocolate bar, a trip to Jamaica is not required, although I suspect it would be eagerly accepted.

> **Fun Fact 80**
>
> Up until the age of six or seven months, a child can breathe and swallow at the same time. An adult cannot do this.

Idea 81: A surprise left in the house when you are away

Details

Surprises work well simply because your partner does not see them coming. We have used a number of methods to make that occur, but there are always others. For this idea, you will need another gift of some sort (flowers, candy, new carpet), and an individual you can trust. Ask this trustworthy person to place or install the item(s) while you and your partner are away from the house.

When you return home from your outing, there the surprise will be. The duration of your absence largely will determine the nature of the gift waiting for her. If you are popping out for a quick coffee, then it will be impractical to attempt to repaint the upstairs. However, if you are heading away for a summer vacation, returning home to something of that nature will be wonderful.

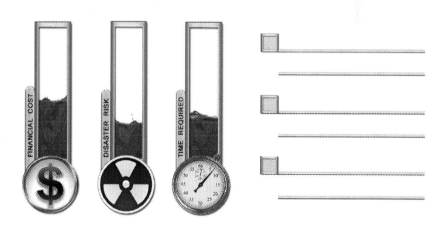

Pitfalls

There is one most conspicuous pitfall here. Make certain the person coming into your house when you are not present is someone you trust implicitly. Nothing kills the effect that flowers might have when they are placed on the floor because all the furniture is gone.

Extras

Take your partner somewhere engaging; a vacation is great, but dinner will suffice. That way, the item left at home for her will be the icing on a very appreciated cake.

Fun Fact 81

Albert Einstein was offered the presidency of Israel in 1952, but he declined.

Idea 82: Messages on the eggs in the carton

Details

Eggs are not solely for eating (just ask a chicken). However, we are not going to warm and hatch an egg. Instead, we are going to use a felt-tip marker to make wonderfully happy faces or write messages on the eggs in the fridge. For the greatest impact, make the bottom row a set of faces, and the top row the things each one is saying; add the standard comic strip speech bubble too. Make it look nice.

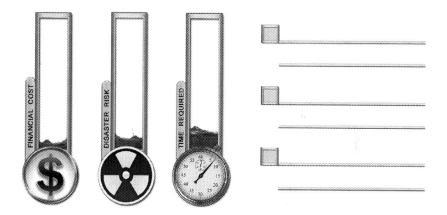

Pitfalls

You never eat eggs? Or you wrote something terrible on them, and it won't come off? You dropped the carton? The chickens wouldn't give them up without a fight?

Extras

Cook her breakfast one morning, and bring it to her in bed. Everyone loves to be pampered and this is one way to do that, which many don't get to enjoy outside a hospital (and that is not fun). If she needs to be the one to sleep in for this to work, make it happen.

Fun Fact 82

In Alaska, it is considered an offense to push a live moose out of a moving airplane. However, once it lands, who is going to know the difference?

Idea 83: A picture on a filled coffee mug

Details

Apply a good photo of you (or the both of you) to a coffee mug. Most photo-development stores offer this service. Then, fill the mug with candy that she enjoys, or use it the next time you bring her a cup of coffee or tea. Add a message on the reverse side of the cup for added impact. Whether she works outside or inside the home, there is always a need for something of this nature.

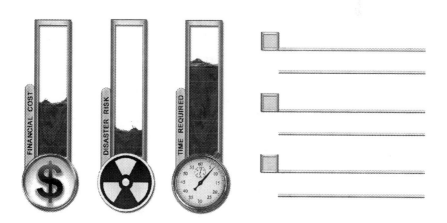

Pitfalls

Select the appropriate picture. Let me say that again: choose wisely. If not, the mug will end up in the trash or way, way, way back in the cupboard. I am sure it was hilarious when you tried on the Speedo, but it's unlikely that your bride will want to look at that first thing in the morning (or ever). Also, do not bring her coffee if she drinks only tea.

Extras

Instead of a regular mug and photo, consider engraving a verse or poem onto a wine glass or glass mug. That will increase the quality of the presentation and how graciously it is received. This works well for anniversaries, of course, but anytime is the correct time to show her your love.

Fun Fact 83

"Warning, cape does not enable user to fly."
on the packaging for a Superman costume

Idea 84: A "bad day" box

Details

Once again, this idea requires some planning and preparation. It also requires a decorative box and a set of envelopes. In each envelope, write a message of support, love, or affirmation. Poems, short verses, song lyrics, and spiritual passages all function well as content. Seal each envelope and place it in the box. When she is having a difficult or bad day, she can open a random envelope and receive a boost from the message inside.

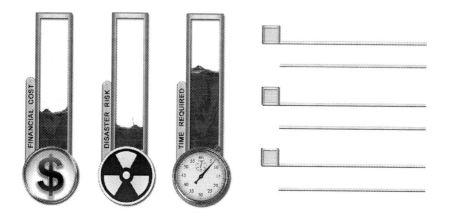

Pitfalls

Make sure the envelopes fit in the box without folding. Keep the presentation as pristine as possible. Put something with meaning on the notes. Writing "Suck it up, Princess!" is unlikely to boost her spirits. For this scheme to work, take some time with it. Compose your messages for her over a period of several days, if required. Think about the kinds of things you would like to hear when you are feeling down.

Extras

Do this right, and it will be enough. A gesture such as this one has long-term impact.

Fun Fact 84

US president Franklin Pierce was arrested during his term for running over an old lady with his horse, but the charges were later dropped. She was not able to testify, for some reason.

Idea 85: Never-fading flowers

Details

This plan is admittedly cheesy, but it should still generate a favorable effect. Purchase a bouquet of eleven roses; buy twelve, and donate one to the checkout guy or gal. Also get a silk rose that looks as much like the real flowers as possible. Wrap them up, and present the bouquet to your partner along with a card, and this is the key: On the card, write "I will love you until the last rose fades." Of course, one rose will not fade.

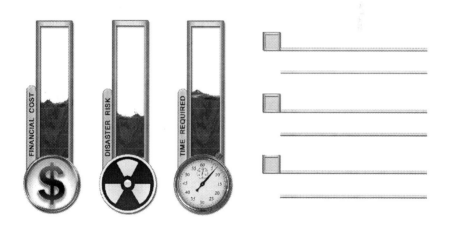

Pitfalls

If you forget to include a silk rose, and all the flowers die within three to five days, you have manufactured significant trouble for yourself. If the silk one somehow gets removed, destroyed, stolen, burned, torn, melted, shredded, trashed, tossed, borrowed, stripped, or otherwise damaged, you will have to do some quick thinking. Other than that, this plan should work.

Extras

Keep that one rose "alive!" And tell her that you love her on a regular basis, etc., etc., etc.

Fun Fact 85

You share your birthday with at least nine million other people in the world. You share your un-birthdays with a whole lot more.

Idea 86: A "survival pack"

Details

At some stage in a relationship, one of you likely will head off somewhere without the other. I am not referring to an excursion to the supermarket, but a trip for business or pleasure that leaves one of you at home. This is a perfect time to create a "survival pack" for your partner, regardless of whether she is leaving or staying, although if she is off on holiday and you are at home with the children, it is evident who needs the kit more. Nevertheless, you should do the presenting, not the receiving.

The pack consists of a small box, a letter or card, some of her favorite things to eat or drink, something small and stuffed, etc. Determine the number of items in the box based on the length of the separation. Ideally, each one should be individually wrapped. Tell your partner to open them in a specified order, at dictated intervals.

My partner first did this for me during our dating years. It still brings a smile to my face, almost twenty years later.

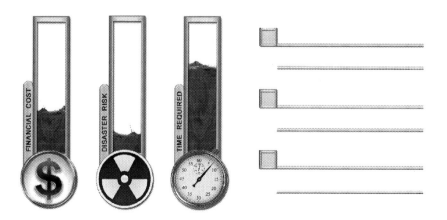

Pitfalls

Do not fill the survival pack with things like ice cream, meat (unless it is dried), or anything else that will stink, spill, or spoil. Make sure she and not the kids, dog, or in-laws opens the box. Gradually increase the value and potential enjoyment of the items she unwraps. It would be unwise to place a diamond ring in the first gift and have the rest contain only a single piece of candy.

Extras

You can go quite a long ways with this idea. Knock yourself out (no, not literally!).

Fun Fact 86

Donkeys kill more people annually than plane crashes ... mostly because they do not fly so well.

Idea 87: A song (and dance) on a music player or earphones

Details

This simple plan is a great one to pull out of your bag of tricks when you are away together (whether or not you are on holiday). Put a favorite song on a music player of your choice and bring along a set of ear-bud headphones. In a place where you would not typically dance—but not where you might get arrested for doing so—place one of the ear pieces in your ear and the other in your partner's, and dance to the music together. If you have access to a headphone splitter that allows the two of you to enjoy the music in full stereo, so much the better.

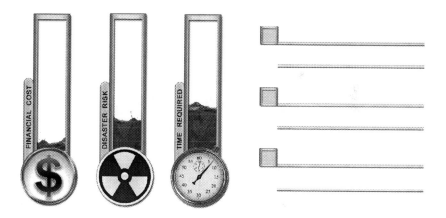

Pitfalls

Pick an appropriate song for a slow dance (not something by Eminem, Metallica, or Tupac). Make sure the player is sufficiently charged. Do not try to do a wild ballroom dance, since you are more likely to choke the two of you with the earphone cord than have a romantic moment. A slow dance. A slow piece of music.

Extras

Doing this on a mountaintop or somewhere extra special will get you plenty of bonus points. Combine this idea with a dinner out or a similar activity.

Fun Fact 87

Alexander the Great and Julius Caesar were both epileptic. This did not seem to hurt their careers any.

Idea 88: An urgent message

Details

Whether your partner is at home or work during the daylight hours, this idea should work equally well.

Using wax crayons or pencil crayons, take a piece of paper and draw a simple picture for your mate. Create a light-hearted scene featuring the two of you, and write a simple love note. Do not fret if you cannot sketch adequately. This should look like a child's drawing, so a fully grown man ought to be able to handle it.

When your masterpiece is completed, insert it into a large envelope and have it couriered to her. Mark the front of the envelope as follows:

Urgent!

For the immediate attention of

[partner's name]

[partner's home or work address]

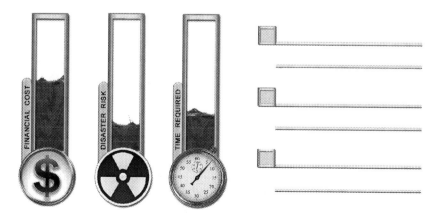

Pitfalls

You should be able to accomplish this plan without any undue grief. The one limiting factor might be the cost of the courier, especially if you're looking for same-day service. However, plan this in advance, and it can arrive a week after you send it. It is not important that she know precisely when you began working on each romantic plot.

Extras

The envelope can include more than just the drawing. However, the strength in this idea rests in its simplicity and the juxtaposition of an urgent delivery and a simple love note.

You also might try to draw out your partner's inner child when at home. Do something light-hearted and fun. Laughter is an ingredient that should be liberally applied to your marriage.

Fun Fact 88

Unless you have a doctor's note, it is illegal to buy ice cream after 6:00 p.m. in Newark, New Jersey. Brain freeze is taken very seriously there.

Idea 89: Helium balloons

Details

Despite my earlier warnings about inhaling helium, I don't want to rule this wonderful substance out altogether. In fact, it is required for this next idea.

Purchase a selection of helium balloons and stuff them into the trunk of the car. Below them, place a large piece of paper or cardboard with a large and bright message: "I love you!"

This surprise can be discovered by your partner in any variety of ways. Perhaps it will spring out when she places her work materials into the car in the morning or when she puts the groceries in the trunk. Or request that she get something for you from the trunk. You should be able to manufacture the circumstances necessary for this to work.

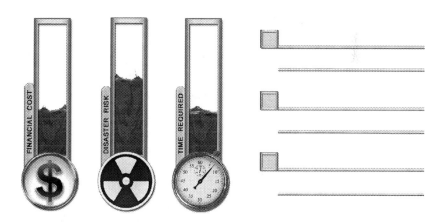

Pitfalls

This idea can be somewhat tricky. The key lies in getting the balloons into the trunk, without them escaping into the atmosphere ahead of schedule. Cars with flip-down seats work best as you can insert the balloons into the trunk without opening it.

Attempt this setup when your partner is not available to observe it.

Finally, if your spouse has a heart condition and reacts poorly to surprises of this nature, consider abandoning this idea and placing a number of floating balloons inside the house instead.

Extras

The place in which the balloons are discovered can greatly increase the impact. You also may consider placing more than a short message below the balloons, such as more expensive items like jewelry or even a favorite type of book.

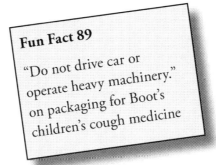

Fun Fact 89

"Do not drive car or operate heavy machinery." on packaging for Boot's children's cough medicine

Idea 90: ????

Details

If, after all this time, you cannot envision a single idea on your own, shame on you.

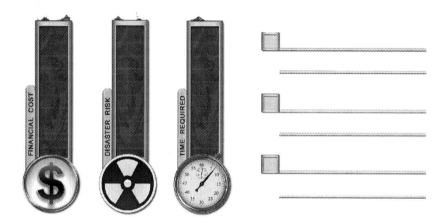

Pitfalls

There are too many possible pitfalls to mention, but since you are a master faker by now, none of them will thwart your plans.

Extras

Your rewards are pride and self-respect, and the realization that you are truly a lover and partner of the highest order.